Profitable Real Estate Investing

Roger Woodson

DEARBORN™
A **Kaplan Professional** Company

This publication is designed to provide accurate and authoritative information in regard to the subject matter covered. It is sold with the understanding that the publisher is not engaged in rendering legal, accounting, or other professional service. If legal advice or other expert assistance is required, the services of a competent professional person should be sought.

Acquisitions Editor: Jean Iversen
Managing Editor: Jack Kiburz
Interior Design: Lucy Jenkins
Cover Design: Salvatore Concialdi
Typesetting: the dotted i

Library of Congress Cataloging-in-Publication Data

Woodson, R. Dodge (Roger Dodge), 1955–
    Profitable real estate investing / Roger Woodson.
       p.   cm.
    Includes bibliographical references and index.
    ISBN 0-7931-3180-4 (pbk.)
    1. Real estate investment—United States.   I. Title.
HD255.W66   1999
332.63′24—dc21   99-17445
                                                       CIP

Dedication

This book is dedicated to Adam, Afton, and Tori, the people who make my life most enjoyable.

ONTENTS

PREFACE

Real estate is one of the most popular investments available because land and buildings have endured many financial storms over the past decades. Investors know that most real estate investments gain value over time. Though the market is cyclic, most properties appreciate, even in bad economic years. In the long run, real estate almost always pays off for patient investors. And real estate is an investment accessible to the average person.

You can use real estate to make fast cash, to build for your retirement, or to accomplish both at the same time. Most investments have trouble keeping up with the rate of inflation. In many cash investments, the value of the investment diminishes greatly as years pass and the money's time value is calculated. This is rarely the case with real estate. Rental properties allow for rental increases as the cost of living goes up. While mortgages usually remain static in cost and are eventually paid off, rental income tends to increase each year. Over a 20-year period, this can amount to major retirement income, especially when an investor owns several income-producing properties.

The Taxpayer Relief Act of 1997 enhanced the appeal of investing in real estate when it lowered the capital gains tax rate. This means a lot to property owners who sell some of their holdings. For example, only 25 percent of real estate depreciation can be recaptured and treated as capital gain. A property sold now is subject to no more than a 20 percent tax rate for capital gains if the seller has owned the property for at least 18 months. A maximum tax rate of 18 percent applies to properties acquired after December 31, 2000, that have been held for more than five years at the time of sale. There's some juicy stuff here that makes real estate deals more attractive than they have been since the tax law changes of 1986.

The right real estate pays for itself. Buildings with positive cash flow are available to investors who know what to look for, where to look for it, and how to recognize it when they find it. This book will show you how to turn up and acquire profitable real estate investments, even if you have no previous experience in the field. You can find many books and seminars that paint a get-rich-quick picture of real estate. While it is quite possible to profit immediately with real estate, the focus here is a successful, balanced, risk-reduced portfolio. In other words, the suggestions are presented to help you become a wise investor who will profit for years to come.

The author, Roger Woodson, is a seasoned real estate investor who is licensed as a designated broker, the highest license classification available in the business. With more than 20 years of experience as both a hands-on investor and broker, his words of wisdom are invaluable. This is your chance to learn from his mistakes, take the shortcuts he has learned, and see exactly how you can make money now and build a retirement income for yourself at the same time.

Woodson has packed these pages with proven procedures for making it as a real estate investor. Afraid you can't get into the game because you don't have a lot of cash? You won't need a lot of money to get your piece of the action. Worried about your credit rating? Woodson presents various ways to participate as a real estate investor regardless of your credit history. Want to make $10,000 in less than a month simply by putting a property under contract yet never actually owning it? Woodson tells you how one of his clients did just this.

All in all, this book is like a treasure map for anyone looking to make money in real estate. Take a few moments to review the table of contents. Flip through the chapters and see for yourself how reader-friendly the text is. Woodson hasn't left anything out, and he presents his advice in easy-to-understand terms with realistic vision.

You no longer have a good excuse for waiting to get into real estate investment. This book is your ticket to a rewarding career, so don't procrastinate a moment longer. Now is the time to make your mark on the world of real estate.

CHAPTER 1

Why Invest in Real Estate?

Not everyone enjoys real estate as an investment, but for those who do, the rewards can be substantial. You can start as a real estate investor with very little cash and turn a shoestring investment into a major money source. Real estate offers fierce competition, tremendous potential profits, and unabating excitement. Adults of any age can play the real estate game, at many different levels of involvement. Some investors are active as landlords, while others take passive positions and simply watch their money grow. Regardless of the path you choose, there is money to be made in real estate.

Real Estate Values Have Withstood the Tests of Time

Real estate is one of the oldest and wisest investments available today. If you look back in history, you can see distinctly how important real estate has been to both people and the economy over the years. Shelter is a natural need for human existence, as is the land shelter is built upon. The ownership of land and buildings has long been a sign of power and wealth. Whether you think of a cattle rancher who owns thousands of acres and most of the water rights in a territory or an investor who owns a top-producing shopping mall, you think of a person with power and money. Historically, those who have controlled land and buildings have enjoyed higher standards of living. The same fact is true today.

Land is one commodity that is no longer being produced. The amount of land the world offers, though abundant, is finite. And much of it currently is being used and simply is not available for sale. Raw land is rarely considered a great investment, but it can be, under the right circumstances. Existing buildings can offer investors tremendous opportunities for rich rewards, and constructing new buildings is always a possibility for profits. In the past, land ownership was a sign of distinction, and a person's power often was figured in terms of the amount of land he owned. This still can be the case today, but a small piece of land in the right place can be worth far more than a lot of land in a less desirable location.

Much has changed in the world of real estate over the last hundreds of years. When people sought shelter in caves, they didn't read classified ads or look for For Rent signs to obtain their living space. Even so, the possession of a fine cave was something to be proud of and easily could mean the difference between living and dying. Today's investors have a huge number of tools at their disposal to make buying, managing, and selling real estate profitable ventures.

Understanding the Cycles of Real Estate

Real estate is cyclical. Many businesses have their ups and downs, and real estate is no exception. However, real estate usually rebounds and grows in value after a slump in appreciation. Historically, many solid real estate investments have depreciated for a period of time, but then have grown again in value. This is not unlike the stock market. Stocks can level off or dip down, but the good ones continue to grow when patient investors hold onto them. Because real estate is a cyclic business, the timing of investments is everything in the early stages of investing. Those who hit the market at the right time can become quite wealthy in a short period of time. Conversely, getting into the market at the wrong time can be an extreme hardship for investors with little cash reserve and may drive the investors to bankruptcy. Spinning your wheel for fortune in real estate is not an activity to be taken lightly.

People who invest in real estate often have diversified portfolios. This allows them to weather storms in the market and come out on top. But people just getting into the real estate market don't have the protection that seasoned investors with broad portfolios have. Making the right decisions early in your investing career is critical. Some people feel that they should start as real estate investors by purchasing single-family homes. This may seem sensible, due to the lower cost of houses compared to other types of real estate, but single-family homes are often a poor choice as first investments. The cash flow generated by a single-family home rented out to tenants usually is not enough to carry the investment's expenses. There are other risks in investing in single-family homes and reasons why houses are not a great place to start—unless you will live in the house—but we will talk more about them later.

Small apartment buildings—those with four or fewer rental units—often are an ideal place for a beginning investor to start on the path to prosperity. Some investors do best when they pool their resources and work with partners to make real estate work for them. You have dozens and dozens of ways to make money with real estate. Some of them are safer than others, and some pay larger dividends than others. Regardless of where investors fit into the market mix, they all must be aware that real estate is not always a stable money maker, but that it usually rebounds when given enough time.

I've worked with real estate for almost 25 years, and I've seen a lot of changes in the market and in financial and real estate trends. As a younger man, I built an extensive portfolio of rental properties that I anticipated would support me in my retirement. The trend at the time was to leverage buildings as much as a lender would allow you to, take the tax deductions, and let inflation help you out on the high loan amounts. The system worked very well for awhile, but then, in 1986, the tax laws changed. In addition to developing my personal portfolio, my business involved building new homes for investors to buy for tax advantages. The change in the tax laws ruined my retirement plans and strained my business because far fewer people bought leveraged buildings for tax shelters after 1986. Not being one to give up, I changed strategies and moved ahead.

When I first moved to Maine, the local real estate market was peaking. It had boomed for years and teetered on the verge of collapse. People from outside the state of Maine had been willing to pay extremely high prices for certain properties. This drove up most market prices. When the market peaked and fell, however, the plummet was substantial. Real estate rarely goes way down in value. In most cases, it appreciates annually or, at the worst, levels off or loses a little ground. In the late 1980s in Maine, the market dropped hard. A glut of homes on the market created economic depreciation, a term real estate appraisers use to say that too many existing homes are on the market. The result of this downturn was disastrous for many homebuilders and investors.

For Example . . .

To give you an idea of how economic depreciation works, let me tell you about a home I built for myself in Maine. When I constructed the house, it was appraised at a cost to build of $185,000. It cost me about $120,000 to build it as a general contractor. In a good market, if I had planned to sell the house, my profit potential would have been $65,000. However, due to the market conditions during construction, economic depreciation pulled the value of the home down to $165,000. In simple terms, I lost $20,000 of equity or potential profit because the market was overloaded with existing homes for sale that were not selling. For a full-time homebuilder, such losses would be enough to make the person rethink his or her line of work. Every investor has different feelings about how much return is enough. In my case, the $45,000 I gained for less than three months of work was adequate. ■

Real Estate Investments Grow by Compounding Value

The compounding value that is normal with most real estate is a factor that makes many investors flock to purchase real property. With the exception of certain markets and some economic times, real estate usually appreciates annually. The percentage of increased value normally is tied, at least somewhat, to the rate of inflation and the cost-of-living index. An appreciation rate of 5 percent a year is not uncommon, and real estate can appreciate much faster. The rate of inflation changes often and is difficult to predict. In any investment, inflation is a factor. Real estate normally keeps pace with inflation and often stays ahead of it. However, at times, the market is flat. To predict your return on an investment, you must set some figure for the rate of inflation. Talk to your local lender, financial adviser, or CPA to arrive at a viable number to use in your personal projections. To illustrate the effect that the inflation rate has on an investment, let's look at a quick example of what might happen when an investor buys a four-unit apartment building in a market where a steady growth of 5 percent a year is expected.

Assume that the investor purchases the apartment building for $200,000. At the end of one year, the building is worth $210,000. By the end of the second year, the building is worth $220,500. In the third year, the value rises to $231,525. The fourth year gain pushes the building's value to $243,101. When the end of the fifth year rolls around, the building is worth $255,256. Over the course of five years, the owner of the building has seen a market price increase of more than $55,000. And the mortgage on the building has been paid down, hopefully with a positive cash flow, during the five years. With enough properties performing like the one in this example, an investor could enjoy a nice profit each year of ownership. ■

Not all real estate appreciates at the same rate. For example, single-family homes usually have higher rates of appreciation than large apartment buildings. But the value of a property when it is acquired affects the paper profit of appreciation. If the building in the example above had been worth $135,000 when the investor purchased it, the profit would not have been as great. A larger building worth $450,000 that appreciated at a rate of only 3 percent would have produced higher profits, even though the rate of appreciation was lower.

Real Estate Is an Excellent Hedge against Inflation

Most investments involve rates of return. If you put money in a bank and collect interest, you will make money, but you may not make as much money as you will lose to inflation. The same can be true with stocks, bonds, mutual funds, and other cash-return investments. Some types of real estate offer investors a better angle to work—the rental angle.

Once real estate is purchased, the purchase price is locked in; it does not go up or down. So assuming that an investor obtains a fixed-rate mortgage, the cost of ownership, in terms of the mortgage, remains the same during ownership. Other costs of ownership, however, fluctuate. For example, property taxes likely will increase. And the cost of utilities normally increases. While these and other costs of ownership do go up, these fluctuations are not all bad. If you own property that you rent to tenants, you can increase the amount of the rent charged to offset increased operational costs. It doesn't have to take long for a building to pay for itself, increasing in value and ultimately (when the mortgage is paid off) leaving you with a cash cow. Long-term investments in the right properties can do very well, indeed. The ability to raise rents is a key factor in why real estate pays off so well in the long run.

Although most investors plan on annual rental increases when projecting a building's profitability, investors sometimes choose not to raise the rents for their properties. One reason might be to keep or attract good tenants when the market for quality tenants is tight. Money lost by not increasing a rental rate may be offset by the savings of not having an empty building or the expense of acquiring a new tenant. If the rental market swings in favor of tenants, and it does from time to time, investors may be forced to keep rents static. For example, if more three-bedroom apartments are available for rent than there are people looking to rent them, charging more for the units will be difficult.

People like to own their own homes. When interest rates are low and people are buying housing, the rental market for residential properties can suffer. In contrast, when interest rates are high and people are not buying, the residential rental market can soar. Rental property is cyclical in nature. Usually, you can increase rental rates annually. The increase may be as little as 3 percent or as high as 7 percent or more. However, you could have a year when you have to *lower* rental rates to attract tenants. There are no guarantees, but investors who are able to stay in the rental game for several years usually do well.

Being in a financial position to hold on for a better year makes the difference between winning and losing in the real estate game. Having cash reserves is not absolutely necessary, but establishing such a fund is wise if you want to last long enough as a real estate investor to see giant gains in your financial status.

Use Existing Real Estate to Finance Your Purchase

Using existing real estate as leverage to buy more real estate can be an excellent way to extend an investment portfolio. However, it also can spell big trouble for an investor who overextends himself. If you have ever heard the expression about being land rich and cash poor, you probably are aware that a real estate investor's financial statement can glow with profit, yet the investor may be strapped for cash. While real estate often makes money for its owner each year, extracting the cash can be difficult. Real estate investors don't get yearly dividend checks or weekly paychecks from their profits. The money made often is tied up in the real estate and very difficult to access. One way to deal with this is to use the equity in the property to buy other buildings. Experienced investors are well aware of this process, but many rookie investors do not know what power their equity in other buildings can bring to them.

Financing rules vary greatly from lender to lender. We will talk about financing in later chapters, but we should touch on some points here. Most lenders require an investor to have a maximum loan value of no more than 80 percent of a property's value. In some cases, lenders will not allow an outstanding loan of more than 70 percent of a building's value. Even with conservative lenders, however, investors often can use the equity in other buildings to buy new buildings without a lot of cash. Let me give you an example.

For Example . . .

Assume you want to buy a new building that has a value of $150,000. If the lender will loan up to 80 percent of the value, you will need a down payment of $30,000. This does not have to be in cash. You could pledge a certificate of deposit or some other cash investment as security on the loan. It's also likely that you could pledge equity in another piece of real estate for the down payment. In other words, if you own a piece of property in which you have extensive equity, you probably can use that equity to finance the new building.

Say, for example, you owe $300,000 on a building that is worth $400,000. An 80 percent value of the $400,000 building equals $320,000. The difference between the payoff amount on the existing loan ($300,000) and the 80 percent value of the building ($320,000) is your equity in the property. Therefore, you should be able to use $20,000 as a down payment on a new building. Some lenders are more liberal and will lend even more. But, bottom line, you should be able to get two-thirds of your down payment for the new building from your investment in the existing building. As long as you make solid, money-making deals, this is a great way to go. ∎

The downside to using existing equity to leverage a new purchase is the risk of losing both buildings if you have financial trouble. Both buildings are tied together with companion mortgages, and any default on one building affects the loan on the other. Later chapters will expand on this topic.

Build Wealth for Retirement

Almost everyone dreams of retiring wealthy. Savvy real estate investors have a wonderful chance of seeing this dream come true.

The fiercest enemy of all investors is inflation. When inflation runs higher than the rate of return on investments, the investors do not keep up with the time value of money. What looks like a profit today results in a reduced value in later years, as inflation eats away at the value of money over time. Putting cash into a standard savings account at a bank is a safe investment, but it is hardly very profitable. To make real money, investors must gamble, and real estate has proved to be a healthy gamble with few risks when long-term investors play their cards right.

The annual appreciation of real estate is only one way in which investors create wealth. If property is used for rental purposes, the rental income increases with inflation and allows investors to receive cash at current money rates, rather than seeing their profit devoured by inflation. As time passes, real estate mortgages are paid off, which increases greatly annual profit potential and cash flow.

Investors who start early enough in life and who manage their rental properties well can retire without financial worries. The rental income they receive when they retire is based on the cost of living at that time. Because they have paid off their buildings, the rental income is like a pension. Plus, the properties continue to grow in value during normal economic times. Buying and holding the right buildings for 20 to 30 years is an ideal way to hedge against inflation, to take advantage of tax breaks, and to create a money machine for the latter part of life.

A real estate investor's business survival is related to many factors. Buying and selling at the right prices is key to success in the field. Seeing that rental properties are managed well is another major point of concern when winning is the goal. And one of the most important factors in succeeding as a real estate investor is a diversified portfolio. To expand on this, let's go to the next chapter and see exactly why a varied group of properties makes your investing safer and more profitable.

Creating a
Diversified Portfolio

Often a diversified portfolio sets apart the successful real estate investor from the entrepreneur who fails. The old saying about not putting all of your eggs in one basket applies particularly to real estate investments. Owning more than one property and more than one *type* of property reduces the risk of failure. However, spreading yourself too thin or investing in properties that you are not sure how to handle is certain to cause trouble. Experienced investors have learned how to balance their needs and desires. New investors must give their goals plenty of thought before jumping to sign purchase and sale contracts. Even investors who have a lot of experience in one type of real estate ownership may need help in branching out to other types of real estate. Investors must weigh many factors before making purchases.

Some investors mix their real estate investments with other types of investments, such as stocks or bonds. Certainly nothing is wrong with this strategy, but investors can diversify without leaving the real estate arena. For example, an investor might broaden her multifamily rental property holdings by purchasing some mixed-use buildings (those that combine residential space with commercial space, such as properties with retail stores on the ground level and residential apartments on the second level) or single-family homes. Buying raw land for development is risky business, but it is another way to explore new angles in real estate investing. Before buying anything, however, you need a plan.

Developing an Investment Strategy

Any investor can develop an investment strategy. However, coming up with a winning game plan may require the assistance of experts, including accountants, lawyers, real estate brokers, or even other investors. Investment strategy is a personal decision (in fact, the most important resource necessary to create your investment strategy is your own mind), but many people and some detailed research can provide insightful information that makes it easier to create a blended plan for success. You don't need any fancy equipment to draft your strategy for buying, renting, managing, and selling real estate. A few sheets of paper and a pencil is all you really require, but a calculator and a computer can be quite helpful.

Start by asking yourself some simple questions: For example, why do you want to invest in real estate? Are you looking for a short-term investment that will turn quick money? Or are you building a retirement nest egg? Maybe you want to do both. Exploring your motivations will help you build an appropriate investment strategy.

Now, it's time to get down to business. You need to plot a course from where you are right now to where you want to be at different stages during your investment career. For example, what do you want to buy or control in your first year as an investor? Now set a goal describing where you will be in three years, five years, perhaps seven years, and ten years. Planning beyond this point is probably useless, except to have a general idea of what you hope to accomplish by the time you retire. The market changes so fast that long-term projections probably will not hold solid.

You also need to establish your financial status when setting up your investment plan and project what properties to buy first. Then consider how you will mix and match properties to balance your investment portfolio. You may want to evaluate growth potential, but don't get bogged down in this step too early in your career. If you will buy property that requires management, determine whether you will take an active role in management or whether you will hire a professional management team.

Your proposed investment plan probably will change many times during your investment activities. It is best to follow your plan as closely as possible while it is working, but be willing to adjust it as needed. The real estate market changes, and good investors change with it. Great investors alter their strategies before most investors ever realize a change is needed. The ability to predict the market comes from both experience and extensive research.

Some people don't bother to put their goals and ideas on paper. They feel that the best way to invest successfully is to roll with the punches and play the game on a day-by-day basis. This strategy usually doesn't work very well for very long, however. Investors with written plans are much more likely to realize their goals. Most people can sit down with a few hours of spare time and come up with a basic investment plan. It may take a weekend to finish, but the time investment is well worth the effort.

Explore Your Financial Needs

Projecting your financial needs for getting started as a real estate investor may not be as simple as it first appears. If you think that you can look at your bank balance, then start buying, you are most likely wrong. Unless you are extremely rich, you will need more time to evaluate your financial abilities. If you don't have a lot of cash, however, don't fall into the trap of assuming that you can't invest in real estate until you accumulate more. It's possible to buy real estate with almost no cash money. As a broker, I've helped investors buy apartment buildings of up to 12 rental units with no cash out of pocket. In some cases, the investors have actually left their closings with more money than they went into the deals with. I have also used creative financing to structure this type of deal for myself. It's not always easy to accomplish, and such a deal can be risky, but it can be done. So you see, having a lot of money is not always a requirement when buying real estate.

When you purchase real estate with the help of a bank or another financial institution, the lender usually requires a down payment of some type. This does not mean that the down payment must be cash, but it usually is. The down payment requirement can be as low as 5 percent or less or as much as 30 percent, or more. The typical down payment for residential property where the buyer will reside is 5 percent. The usual requirement for a nonowner-occupied building is 20 percent. Some lenders demand a down payment of 30 percent on investment property. Yet, with owner financing, you might obtain a building with no down payment. No rock-solid rules cover loans that are not sold on the secondary mortgage market. When you borrow money from a source that will sell the loan on the secondary mortgage market, however, the loan requirements are more strict than they might be with portfolio loans.

A portfolio loan is one that is not sold on the secondary mortgage market. Many commercial banks make portfolio loans. Rather than sell the loans, the banks keep and service them. Under the circumstances, a bank has only its own rules to play by, so creative financing is easier to structure. Loans made for buildings with more than four units fall in the commercial loans category. Portfolio loans and commercial loans both can be treated differently than loans that will be sold on the secondary market.

In terms of your investment plan, your financial requirements need not be ironclad. First, list your total cash available for investment. This doesn't mean all the cash you have, but rather the amount you can afford to invest. Next, evaluate your net worth by using a profit-and-loss (P&L) statement. List all of your debts in terms of the total amounts you owe, not the monthly payments. Then list all of your assets in terms of their total value. For example, if your home is worth $200,000 and you owe $150,000 on it, list both figures, then deduct the debt from the assets (yielding $50,000, in this case). The time you devote to accounting for all debts and assets in the P&L will be well spent because you must complete forms that are essentially P&L statements when you apply for a loan.

Once you have a clear picture of your cash on hand and your net worth, consider how much disposable income you have each month. This is important because you may need to make monthly payments, or at least supplement them, once you buy a new property. If you are running on a tight budget with your present financial responsibilities, think long and hard before buying a new property. It is best when you have enough disposable income to make ends meet if your expected cash flow from the new property falls below expected returns.

Selecting Your First Properties

Selecting your first properties is a very important step. If you choose poorly in the beginning, your real estate experience may be bitter. Learning what to look for and when to buy a property are essential to your success. No cookie cutter approach works for all investors. However, most first-time investors do best when they start with small apartment buildings. Duplexes can be good investments for investors who will live in one of the units, but they generally don't produce enough income to pay for themselves when they are not owner occupied. Buildings with four rental units typically are ideal first investments. The cost of these buildings is usually manageable, and the financing often is quite attractive because the buildings can be purchased with as little as a 5 percent down payment when the purchaser will live in one of the units.

A four-unit building offers many advantages over a duplex. If you don't plan to live in the apartment building, you have four rental units to pay for the property. If one unit goes vacant for awhile, you still have three units to help pay the mortgage. It's possible to buy buildings where the three units cover your costs and the fourth unit represents profit. Creative financing usually is not very effective with four-unit buildings because the loans generally are sold on the secondary market and must meet strict criteria.

Triplexes are buildings with three rental units. Normally, they are better than duplexes, but not as good as four-unit buildings. When you make your choices, don't be blinded by the sales price. A cheap building is not always a bargain. You have to run the numbers on any property to see whether it is a viable purchase.

A lot of investors consider buying a single-family house, condo, or co-op as an investment property. This can be okay if you will live in the home, but a single-family dwelling generally is a poor investment for purely financial purposes. The cost of most homes is too high to expect the rental income to cover the cost of the mortgage.

Starting Small

Starting small is not a prerequisite when getting into real estate, but it usually is the best path to take. Entrepreneurs who jump into the market with big investments often struggle. Large projects can require a lot of time, attention, and money. This is true of small buildings, too, but smaller buildings normally are easier for inexperienced investors to work with. Although many investors begin with a four-unit building, starting your real estate career with a six-unit apartment building is acceptable. You probably will notice little difference in the management of a six-unit building compared to that of a four-unit building. The financing can vary significantly, but the day-to-day activities are similar. However, buying a large apartment building—one with 12 or more rental units—or a commercial property requires considerable real estate investment skill.

Each investor must tailor a plan around individual circumstances. It's not fair to say that you must start investing in real estate with a four-unit apartment building. Buying 200 acres of land and developing it into ten-acre building lots might be right up your alley. Investors are as different as the real estate they buy. The key is knowing your limits and working within them. Over time, you can stretch your limits little by little. A wise investor I worked with years ago told me that he measured a deal by deciding what the worst-case scenario would be once he signed the contract. If this scenario would not break him financially and he felt good about the deal, he would pursue it. But if the deal could bankrupt him, he wouldn't close, no matter how good the deal looked. His words are not bad advice.

Expanding to Larger Buildings

Larger buildings typically cost more to purchase and operate than smaller properties. This can make acquiring one difficult in the early stages of real estate investing. After time, it's easy to move up to bigger buildings, when you have good equity levels in other buildings to work with. Tying up too much cash to buy one property usually is not a great idea. There are, of course, exceptions. If you ever played Monopoly as a kid, you know how coveted Boardwalk and Park Place are. They are much more desirable than Baltic Avenue, for example. In many ways, the game of Monopoly is a good introduction to real-life investing. I used to play it a lot. Maybe that's why I've been so involved with real estate as an adult.

Big buildings can mean big money, but they also can mean big problems. Until you gain a few years of experience as a real estate investor, you probably should avoid large properties. Get your routines and contacts worked out first. For example, find good plumbers, electricians, and other service providers before you need them. Establish yourself either as an active property manager or with a professional management firm before you need to handle a lot of rental units. If you have a full-time job and you invest on the side, take your limited time into consideration. For average investors, buildings that have more than 12 rental units are too much to handle in the early stages of developing an investment career in real estate, but can be added to a portfolio in later years, as an investor gains more experience and stability.

Mixing and Matching for Diversity

Mixing and matching property styles and types is an excellent way to diversify your rental portfolio. The first step, however, is to build a strong foundation. For the sake of our example, this foundation will be constructed with small multifamily buildings. Let's assume that you buy a triplex and a four-unit building during your first year or two of your investing career. Your experience with these buildings has been favorable and profitable. You are now ready to move forward with some new types of properties. What will you buy?

A co-op is a risky investment. You don't own actual real estate; instead, you own stock in a corporation that owns real estate. A condo could work, but it's not what most investors consider the wisest move. A single-family home is another option, but still not a great option for most people. A shopping center is far beyond the capabilities of average investors, so it is not an option. Raw land is too risky and too much work for most people. This leaves the next logical step after owning small multifamily buildings: larger apartment buildings. Rental properties with six dwelling units are an excellent choice for investors with moderate experience. Buildings with up to 12 rental units usually are good investments for those who have experience with smaller rental properties.

Another consideration is a property zoned for mixed use. A modest building of this type can be a good stepping stone to commercial properties. When it's time to move forward, you also can consider buying fixer-upper properties and get into rehabilitation (rehab) work. For investors with good organizational skills who are willing to work as general contractors, this can be a very lucrative move. Chapter 13 covers the topic of rehab work completely.

Different Types of Real Estate

You have a host of different types of real estate to invest in. You can buy restaurants, retail space, professional buildings, industrial parks, shopping centers, homes, apartment buildings, land, and a number of other property types. Each investor must match purchases to the individual plan he has developed. My background in construction made me a natural for both land development and fixer-upper properties. Some investors would fail miserably in the fields where I have excelled. The good news is that plenty of opportunity in all forms of real estate allows anyone to find her niche. Match your interest and your skills to the right property types and you should do fine.

For example, assume you are a dentist by profession. You have no experience in construction or remodeling. If you go to an auction and buy an apartment building that was gutted by a fire, you could easily be buying into a nightmare. If I bought the same building, my past experience would help me to see the trouble spots and adjust my bid accordingly. If you were a tax lawyer or a certified public accountant, on the other hand, you most likely would do much better than I in structuring or buying into a real estate investment trust or partnership. Evaluate and use your strengths as you grow your real estate business. If, after all this, you doubt your ability to be a real estate investor, turn to the next chapter for help in determining where you fit into the game.

CHAPTER 3

Should You Be a Real Estate Investor?

Why does real estate as an investment work extremely well for some people and not so well for others? For one thing, personality has some effect on whether a person should be a real estate investor. The experience and background of potential investors also determine who should and who should not be involved in real estate. Are you a candidate for the real estate world? Almost any adult can invest in real estate. However, discovering where you fit into the business end of real estate can require some effort. The work is not hard, but you must develop a personal profile if you want to be successful.

People who dabble in several investment types are rarely big winners. More often than not, specialists prevail in the battle for big bucks. When people concentrate their efforts on a single activity, they usually become quite good at what they do. This is true of sports, business, and investing, among other activities. The amount of work required to be a consistent winner can be substantial. If you must spread your efforts over several types of investments, you likely will not have the time to keep yourself up to date with every hiccup in the market. Some successful investors make their money work for them in varied forms of investments, but most big-league investors find a niche that is comfortable for them and work it to the max. Others use real estate as a part-time income, as a hedge against other investments, or as a career.

Is Real Estate Right for You?

Can you see yourself as a real estate investor? Nearly everyone can invest in real estate, but certain qualities generally exist among seasoned, successful real estate investors. The first question you must answer is whether you want to put your money into real estate. If you weren't somewhat interested in the possibility, you probably would not be reading this book. But maybe you are just curious. Real estate is a big investment that is not always easy to liquidate. If you buy into mutual funds and decide six months later that you don't like what you are doing, for example, you can sell out easily. This is not always the case with real estate. In fact, selling your real estate holdings can take a year or more. Therefore you cannot afford to buy property until you are sure it's what you want to do.

As an investment real estate broker, I have talked with hundreds of investors. Some of them were looking for their first properties to buy, and others were selling their portfolios to move into other types of investments. The first-time buyers often shared a common distinction. When I asked them why they wanted to buy investment real estate, the most frequent answer was no surprise: they wanted to make money. The potential investors often believed that real estate was a hands-off, easy way to earn big bucks. People who think this have been watching too many infomercials! Except for a few exceptions, real estate is not an easy business, and it often requires active participation in some form. Even if she uses a management company to handle day-to-day tasks, the savvy investor remains active in overseeing the management company. So if you believe you can buy an apartment building, then go to the golf course while you make money hand over fist, you had better think again.

Some investors devote only a couple of hours a week to their rental properties, while others spend entire weekends and some nights working with their properties. If you retain a management company to run your buildings, you should need no more than an hour or two a week to stay on top of your investments. However, if you maintain your own buildings, rent out your own vacancies, and take an active role in all aspects of management, even a small residential property can consume hours a week. Usually, the time demands come in waves. It's not the type of work you can budget.

Investors who hold down full-time jobs can manage their own properties, but the task can be demanding. Most management issues can be dealt with after regular business hours; however, some properties require more active management than others. If you have good buildings and good tenants, the properties might run themselves for the most part. However, if you travel a lot in your work, hiring a management company probably will be essential.

You don't have to wear a black overcoat and top hat and sport a long handlebar moustache to be a landlord. It is not necessary to go from door to door on a weekly basis to collect rent, although some landlords do. You can hire a management firm to perform most of your investment duties, but you must be willing to take some part in your investments if you want to see maximum success. In fact, this is true of most investments. People who invest in stocks usually don't buy them, then let them sit, for example. Good investors monitor their investments and make adjustments when the market shifts. And real estate often requires more effort than straight financial investments.

You have many factors to consider when weighing your decision to become a real estate investor. Are you willing to put up with the hassles of rental property? Does the thought of developing land excite you? Would commercial real estate suit you better than residential real estate? Can you see yourself as a stockholder of a co-op housing development? Does the idea of pooling your money with that of other investors then using the joint money to buy an expensive piece of real estate appeal to you? The list of potential questions you could ask yourself is endless. But you must address certain questions if you want to be successful, so let's concentrate on them.

What Are Your Goals?

First, determine your goals and desires as a real estate investor. Various levels of real estate investment strategy exist. For instance, some people want a quick return on their money—perhaps a profit within a year's time. Other investors expect their real estate investments to pay off in five to seven years, a very practical approach. Still other investors buy real estate as a means of retirement income. All three types of investors can meet their goals with real estate. And it's even possible to mix and match purchases to enjoy success at all three levels of investment strategy.

So set aside some time to think about your goals in life and how investing in real estate will affect them. If you are a parent of a young child, for example, you might look to real estate as a means of creating a college fund for your child. Or you might want to use real estate to build wealth for your later years. Or perhaps you are a person who buys real estate to make money, but also because you enjoy the business. I'm one of these people. My grandfather got me interested in real estate when I was very young, and the lure of the land has never gone away. Because everyone has individual tastes, goals, and desires, you must address yours personally.

Things in life that are planned often work out better than things that are done spontaneously. Therefore, if you want to invest in real estate, you should create a plan, a goal. Let's say, for example, that at 30 years old, you are interested in creating a retirement plan for yourself. Investing in an individual retirement account (IRA) is one way to build for the future. Other cash investment plans also can help create a retirement fund. But real estate certainly is one of the most lucrative vehicles you can use to cruise into your golden years.

For Example . . .

Let's take our example further. Investors often finance their rental properties for 20 years. If you are 30 years old when you finance your first building for 20 years, you will pay off the building when you are 50 years old. If you buy one building each year until you are 45 years old, you will have 15 buildings that will all be paid for when you are 65 years old. If each building contains six rental units—a good number of units to have for both profit and ease of management—you will have 90 apartments to support you when you retire. Assuming that the present rent for each apartment is $675 per month, that's $729,000 a year in today's money. Of course, you will incur expenses for management and operation, and you have a mortgage to pay off over the first 20 years of ownership. But when you retire at age 65, you would have the lion's share of that $729,000 a year as income. Best of all, the rents will continue to increase with inflation, so by the time you retire, the income will be much, much higher and it will counterbalance the rate of inflation. Your IRA and other cash investments don't have this kind of power. Also remember, we stopped buying in our example at age 45, but you could possibly continue to buy for many more years afterward. ■

Let's assume that you are not worried about retirement income at this stage of your life. You probably should be planning for it, but we will agree that your focus is on buying a large parcel of land to accommodate your own horse ranch. To do this, you need money—

and lots of it. So you look for a way to turn a few thousand dollars into tens of thousands of dollars in a hurry. Real estate can meet this goal, too. Under this scenario, you are a prime candidate for what I call quick-flips—that is, deals you buy and sell within a year or two. We will talk about many types of quick-flips in a later chapter. For now, we will concentrate on one type of quick-flip.

For Example . . .

Certain properties on the market are ripe for picking. These properties have hidden potential that a wise investor can cash in on. To illustrate this example, let me tell you about a real-life deal that benefited a number of people. A large two-family duplex was on the market for sale. The real estate brokerage that listed the building had been trying to sell it for more than a year. As an investment broker, I dug into the details on the property and discovered that the zoning for the building allowed use by up to five families. When the listing agreement expired with the unsuccessful brokerage, I contacted the property owner and listed the building for my brokerage to sell at $10,000 more than it had been offered for sale previously. The owner was skeptical because a big-name agency couldn't sell it after a year at a lower price, but I was confident.

Once I had the listing in hand, I called one of my regular investors and told him about the property and about my discovery. In less than a week, the investor put the property under contract. Within two weeks, I helped the investor find someone who offered to buy his contract. The seller made a quick sale and a higher profit than he ever expected. My first investor made about $10,000 in less than a month for putting the property under contract, then selling his rights to the contract. The second investor changed the building from two units to four units, split the land to obtain an additional building lot to sell, as I had advised, and made a large profit in less than a year. Everyone in the deal made money quickly. When I saw the raw potential, I simply put the wheels in motion. Deals like this don't come along every day, but they do exist. In fact, in a good year I handle several of them. ■

If you want to build up money to pay for your child's college education, you can do it with the mid-range plan, assuming you have a few years to work with before you need the cash. In this situation, you would buy buildings with the intent of keeping them for between three and seven years, then selling them. During these years, you hope that the properties' appreciation rates increase their values. You know that the rental income should rise each year, and that makes the numbers for the buildings work better on a spreadsheet. Setting a goal like this is very realistic and usually is quite safe.

How Much Effort Will You Invest?

Another key question in determining how successful you will be as an investor is this: How much effort are you willing to invest in working with real estate? For example, if you are thinking of buying rental property, there can be a lot more work involved with the process than you might think. To make this clear, let's look at some of the responsibilities of owning a six-unit apartment building. Many of the day-to-day activities we are about to discuss can be handled by a property management firm, but keep in mind, management companies often charge 10 percent of a property's gross income, plus other fees, for their services.

When you own an apartment building, many tasks must be attended to. You can do some, even most, of them yourself, or you can hire people to take care of the work for you. If you hire people to do the job, you will recover less profit at the end of the year. However, you have to factor in what your time is worth. It may be less costly for you to pay someone else to manage your properties than it would be to take time away from your earning capacity. Once you acquire a building, it may need some immediate maintenance or repairs. If not, this type of work certainly will be required over time. Are you handy with tools? Will you do some of the work yourself? Do you have time to call contractors and meet them to schedule work you are not qualified to do? Not all buildings require a lot of attention in terms of maintenance and repair, but some do.

Every landlord knows that tenants make the world go around. Will you design, write, and place your own advertisements for tenants when you must fill an empty apartment? Can you be available to show the apartment to prospective tenants at various times during the day and evening? Does it frighten you to meet strangers after just one phone call? Are you equipped to screen the tenants, pull credit reports on them, check references, and do your best to get good tenants? Showing and renting apartments can be time consuming when you own several buildings or even one larger property.

Still other responsibilities exist. Who will cover the move-in and move-out checklists? Will you be able to evict tenants who don't pay their rent? Speaking of rent, how do you plan to collect it? Will tenants mail it in, or will you pick it up? What actions will you take when tenants don't pay their rent on time? Who will you call in the middle of the night when a plumbing pipe bursts and floods your building?

Are you starting to get the picture? Managing rental properties is not easy work. Even if you hire a management company to do most of the work for you, not all management companies do their jobs as well as you might like. For this reason, a successful investor monitors his management company carefully. Any way you look at it, handling rental properties is not stress free.

Before you buy into real estate, give some serious thought to just how much effort you are willing to expend for your profits. If you want to contract most of the work out to others, buy only buildings that have strong enough numbers to support your expenses. Of course, this will limit your portfolio significantly in terms of the buildings that will suit your needs.

What Is Your Personality Profile?

Your personality plays an important role in how successful you are in real estate. Real estate opportunities exist to fit most personalities, but it is up to you to determine which options work best for you. For example, if you don't enjoy dealing with people, seek real estate deals where you can rely on management companies or brokers to handle the people skills. Investors who dislike conflicts and court dates might not make good landlords for certain property types. If your organizational skills are sketchy, plan on hiring someone to work with you in your new venture. Do you hate when the phone interrupts your dinner or wakes you from a deep sleep? Landlords get calls at all hours, so plan on having some help if you are unwilling to accept the annoyance and the responsibility of phone calls outside of normal business hours.

Investors who enjoy working with people have a good chance of becoming successful landlords. What type of people do you work with best? Are you more comfortable with entrepreneurs in business suits who rent professional space, or do you prefer working with families looking for nice places to live? If you don't enjoy working with the public, but like to associate with contractors and business contacts, you might do well as a developer.

Take a long look at yourself. Do some role playing. Ask yourself questions pertaining to different types of responsibilities in real estate. Write your answers on paper, and review them. These mental exercises will help you pinpoint the types of real estate that you should look for. Once you have narrowed the field, you can begin to concentrate on becoming successful in your chosen endeavors.

Becoming an Astute Investor

Learning to be an astute real estate investor is not complicated, but it does require some commitment. You've taken a good step in reading this book. In fact, reading and research are two tools that no successful investor ignores. Even when you reach the pinnacle of your investing profession, you have more to learn. Real estate evolves, and you must keep up with the ongoing changes. People who think they know all that they need to know find themselves left behind as the years roll by. All investors owe it to themselves to stay on top of their chosen investments. In real estate, this can mean many things. For example, you must stay abreast of current rental rates and adjust yours as needed. Investors who own property that is leased for business purposes may have to update the wiring in their buildings to accommodate new technology and tools. An investor into land development must keep up with ecological laws and zoning changes. The task of staying informed never ends for successful real estate investors.

History can teach you volumes in terms of strategies for real estate. We know that real estate is a cyclical business and that history often repeats itself. These factors point to the assumption that by studying past performances, past trends, and other elements of historical documentation, it is possible, at least to some extent, to predict the future of real estate. If you are truly committed to real estate, you will dig deep into old newspapers, books, tax records, and anything else you can find to determine how to chart your course in the investment world. Research and education are your two best tools when you deal in real estate.

Honing the Edge of Investment Strategy

Honing the edge of your investment strategy is not difficult. With the right research, you can be up and running in just a few months. Take some time to do your reading and to research what you want to do before you do it. You may spend six months preparing for your first purchase. Take a year if you need it. But be well-prepared mentally before you step into the real estate arena. Learn what options are available to you. Decide what opportunities match your needs and personality best. Investigate financing angles and marketing maneuvers. Don't squander your time, but allow yourself an adequate amount of preparation before you buy property.

Once you own real estate, getting rid of it can be difficult and time consuming. If you make a bad purchase, you will have trouble finding someone to take it off your hands. Real estate is not like a car, whose value drops dramatically once it is purchased; however, a bad deal is still hard to sell, but easy to buy. Don't buy something just because you can afford it or because the deal seems too good to be true. Think before you act. Make wise buying decisions. Try to avoid buying something you will regret. Real estate usually is not an easy turnover game. It is far better to put off purchasing a property while you evaluate it more thoroughly than it is to buy it, then wish you hadn't. Preparation for your new venture as an investor is the best insurance you can have for avoiding the pitfalls that many rookies get sucked into.

CHAPTER 4

Short-Term Money Makers

Investors usually love buying and selling—especially when they make a nice profit. Certain opportunities in real estate make it possible to buy and sell buildings quickly for staggering profits. This is part of the lure of the game. Making tens of thousands of dollars for a few months of part-time management is exciting. Can people really make big money in real estate? Absolutely. Is it possible to make a lot of money in less than a year when working with real estate? No doubt about it. Once a person knows what to look for and what to do, the amount of money she can make in a year or two with real estate is almost unbelievable.

Property Types That Can Earn Big Money

People who want to see fast returns on their money in real estate don't always know what type of property to buy. Not all real estate is suitable for a quick sale that nets a hefty profit. To make money fast, you need to find what I call quick-flips. A quick-flip is a property that you can buy at a fair price; convert, repair, or restore; then sell it in less than a year for a substantial financial gain. Competition for quick-flips is, as you might imagine, rigorous. Whenever an opportunity exists to make a lot of money in a little time, people flock to it.

Undoubtedly a lot of people will look for the same types of quick-flip properties that you will seek. But a good number of investors are not interested in such deals because they seek properties with different investment strategies in mind. Maybe they don't want to roll up their sleeves and hoist a hammer. Maybe they don't want to go through any zoning changes required to make a property soar with potential. Whatever the reason, some investors simply want to invest in other ways. If you are inclined toward quick-flips, however, they are a proven way to make a lot of money in a short time.

Almost any type of real estate can fall into the quick-flip category. But this is not to say that all real estate is suitable for a quick sale. Let me give you an example.

For Example . . .

Assume that two motels are on the market. One is making a profit and is in good condition. It might be a reasonable long-term investment, but it doesn't show any signs of being a quick-flip target. Now assume that the other motel on the market is old, rundown, and off the beaten path since a new highway has been built. This is not the kind of property you would want to buy to operate as a motel, but it might have some other potential. Maybe you could have the zoning changed from motel to condo status, for example. Then you could rehab the building and convert it into individual condominiums. Accomplishing this successfully with a good marketing plan could generate a huge amount of income. ■

Properties that have something special going for them are best suited to the quick-flip strategy. In some cases, the "something special" is the need for repairs or restoration. Changes in zoning also can make a building a good quick-flip. Property being sold at auction can have quick-flip potential, due to the possibility of buying the property at far below market value. Any type of distress sale also might make a quick-flip deal. The key is to discover something that you can do in a short time to increase a property's value. This can be as simple as buying the property at a bargain price or as complicated as rebuilding a burned-out building.

Finding Quick-Flip Deals

Finding property to buy is easy, but finding property to buy with an intent to resell it soon for a profit is not so simple. Advertisements of real estate for sale in the classified section of a newspaper can be a start, but it is far from all that will be required. Rarely will you see an ad for a property that tells you the property is a prime piece of real estate for a quick profit. You must read between the lines and do a lot of digging to find the hidden wealth in quick-flip deals.

There is no one way or place to find quick-flip properties, but you can start with the following suggestions.

Auctions. Buying from auctions often is one way to get a bargain; however, it can be risky, and most people have difficulty getting enough money together to take advantage of auctions. Properties at auctions sell "as is," and investors may not have enough opportunity to inspect the buildings properly. You have little, if any, chance of using contingency clauses to protect yourself when buying auctioned property. Most property sold at auctions must be paid for in a short time. If you plan to buy at auctions, talk to your lender and establish a line of credit to work with. This is a luxury that most investors who are just starting out cannot take advantage of. If you have extensive assets, however, your lender may give you an open line of credit. Most likely, though, despite your assets, it probably will be difficult to establish such financing until you have a successful track record as an investor.

Real estate brokers. Real estate brokers can help you find quick-flip properties, but often brokers are your biggest competitors. Brokers see what's coming on the market early in the selling process. It is not illegal for them to buy properties for themselves, and many do. But other brokers like me, who specialize in investment properties, will help you find and buy quick-flips. Brokers like these deals because they make money when they sell quick-flip properties and usually make money when the properties are resold. Brokers who participate in Multiple Listing Services—and most do—have access to a large number of various property types.

Contractors. Contractors are another potential source of quick-flip deals. This may seem strange because contractors normally are your competitors, but it's true. At times, contractors overextend themselves financially and must liquidate their real estate quickly and for low prices. If you are in the right place at the right time, you might get the chance to buy a great quick-flip deal from a contractor trying to avoid bankruptcy.

Lenders. Banks can be an excellent source of quick-flips. When lenders foreclose on properties for nonpayment of mortgages, they often resell the properties at very low prices through public notice. With a little work in getting to know the workout officers at the lender (the people in charge of properties whose loans are in default), you might be able to get first refusal on a property where foreclosure is pending. At the very least, you might get some advance notice that a property is coming up for sale.

Real estate professionals. Lawyers often are asked to liquidate properties to settle estates, divorces, and other problems.

Sending letters to local attorneys to let them know you are a viable buyer who can act quickly may get you on lists that produce quick-flip opportunities. Accountants, frequently consulted for financial advice, sometimes are asked about ways to change financial situations. Their advice can result in a decision to sell a property. As with lawyers, letters to accountants may produce some buying opportunities. And if you will be selling investment property that has a cash flow, the accountants may be a source of buyers for your completed projects.

Other opportunities.   Buying property that is being liquidated to settle a bankruptcy or a divorce can produce quick-flip deals. Buildings damaged by fire sometimes can be sweet deals for experienced rehabbers. Any property that can be rezoned for more profitable use, such as a house rezoned for use as office space, can provide quick-flip potential. Raw land usually doesn't offer quick-flip opportunities, but in some cases it can. (I provide an example below.) Most properties suitable for quick-flips are right under the noses of investors who fail to dig deeply enough to see the real value.

For Example . . .

I used to work with an investor who felt that mass transportation was going to be needed from Virginia to Washington, D.C., in the coming years. Based on his belief, the investor put options to buy on a lot of land. Being a land developer and real estate investor, he knew how to structure big deals with very little cash. After securing large tracts of land in suitable locations, the developer worked to bring the need for mass transit to the proper politicians. The process took years, but in the end the developer bought the land he controlled, then sold it for a huge profit to facilitate a route for a commuter train installation. ∎

Any real estate may have potential for a quick flip, so look for hidden value in every ugly duckling property you encounter. After awhile, you will begin to develop a sense of what to look for in various types of property. The amount of time you have available to dedicate to your searches also will affect how successful you are. With enough time and some learned researching skills, you should be able to start spotting quick-flip deals.

How Much Risk Will You Accept?

How much risk do quick-flip deals involve? This is a hard question to answer, but a good one to ask. Many factors affect risk levels. For example, your experience and expertise have great bearing on what risk you will face. The types of properties you choose also affect risk level.

You have three main reasons to be concerned about the risk of quick-flips:

1. What happens if you buy a property, then can't accomplish what you hoped to?   You can eliminate the risk of not being able to accomplish your goals by using contingency clauses in your purchase contract. For example, you might say you are not obligated to buy a property unless your loan for building improvements is approved. Contingency clauses all but eliminate one of the three big risks.

2. What happens if you can't find a buyer for your project when it's completed?   Not being able to find a buyer for your project is a possibility you should prepare for. You can overcome this risk by staying away from projects that you must sell later. In other words, if you buy a duplex and convert it to a triplex, be prepared to keep it as rental property if it doesn't sell for a profit. If you box yourself in financially so that a sale is mandatory, you flirt with bankruptcy. Always leave yourself a safe way to offset a slow sale.

3. What happens if the work being done on your project costs more than it was projected to? Cost over-runs are a problem with any type of construction or remodeling. Most overruns can be controlled with proper management. For example, if you rehab a house, make sure the contracts you enter with the people who will do the work detail specifically what will be accomplished and exactly what the work will cost. Have material suppliers lock in quotes for enough time to complete the job. When you budget your money, build in a safety margin to protect against cost overruns. If you do your job right, you can eliminate nearly all of the risk of quick-flips.

Risk and Reward

In many types of investments, the rewards are related directly to the risk investors take. A safe cash investment in a savings account at a bank will not pay off as much as a high-risk bond. The same principle is true, to some extent, in real estate, but real estate can be made safer. You don't have to be reckless and live in constant risk to make major money in real estate. Learning the ropes is the tricky part. The good news is that hundreds of books, seminars, and training materials are available to dedicated real estate investors. If you are committed to making real estate a career, you can achieve your goal.

"Fast" Is a Relative Term

"Fast" is a relative term in real estate. A fast transaction in real estate, when financing is needed, takes about 60 days or more. A fast sale usually takes less than six months to complete. In other words, getting a contract from someone to purchase property within six months, then having the deal close within two months after the contract is signed, is considered fast. So total time could run about eight months. Now, some deals progress much faster and others go much slower. Real estate offers no guarantees.

People who play the stock market, buy into futures or mutual funds, or use rollover certificates of deposit might consider a month to be fast when closing a transaction, while a real estate investor might think of anything less than a year as being fast. Good real estate investors learn patience early in their careers. They also must be willing to adjust their plans and to make quick decisions to capitalize on market shifts.

Earn while You Learn

Real estate investing can be an "earn while you learn" experience. For example, your first attempt at a quick-flip might result in only a modest financial gain. But as you rack up experience, your profits should increase. As long as you do not lose money, you gain valuable experience that you can harness to make you wealthy in the future. Even if you lose a few thousand dollars on a deal as you learn, you can recover the loss on your next project if the experience helped you perfect your abilities. Experience and dedication can take anyone a long way in the game of real estate investment.

Quick-flips offer the potential for fast money, but they require more time and attention than some other types of real estate. Some investors are more comfortable with different investment strategies. You might find that you prefer a more controlled form of investing. If this is the case, an investment plan based on a moderate holding period for properties might suit you better. Let's turn to the next chapter to see how such a portfolio can change your needs as an investor.

CHAPTER 5

Midterm Keepers

You can make fast money with quick-flip deals, but often you can earn even more money if you are willing to wait a few years to cash in on your earnings. Generally speaking, the longer you hold onto real estate, the more it appreciates in value. This is not the case with every property, and the cycles that real estate goes through can mean that some years will show no financial gains. However, in most cases, real estate values increase over time. This is a good reason to hang onto some properties for at least a few years before selling them. A medium time range may be five years. This gives a property time to increase in value with the appreciation rate and gives you time to boost its value through better management and improvements.

Investors who concentrate only on quick-flips don't tie up their money for very long when things go as planned. Keeping a property for several years, however, means that your money may not be available for quite a while. But it's possible that if you buy the right building and make the right moves, you can borrow money against your equity in the building to keep your cash liquid.

The following sections explore reasons to keep real estate for several years before selling it.

Making a Commitment to Hold onto Real Estate

Making a commitment to hold onto a building for several years is a big decision. If you buy a property that has no quick-flip potential because you plan to keep the building long enough for it to grow in value, you must be prepared for the wait. The years might pass swiftly if you get a nice property that presents few problems during your ownership. By the same token, you could wind up with a building that needs frequent financial and personal attention. If you get a troublesome building years of ownership can be unpleasant. For this reason, investigate thoroughly before you buy a building you intend to keep for several years.

Properties suitable to own for up to ten years are what I call midterm keepers. To me, this means that the properties have good potential for awhile, but they don't have the means to carry you through retirement or add to your portfolio on a long-term basis. The factors used to determine a building's potential investment life vary. In some cases, the deciding factor is the condition of a building. Maybe the mechanical systems have only a year or two left in them before they will need replacement. Another factor might be the status of the neighborhood. If a building's location is peaking, the property's value may decline in later years. On the other hand, if the building is in an area of growth and revitalization, the property could increase in value for many years.

Before you purchase a midterm keeper, determine how much money you could afford to spend on the building's upkeep if it became necessary. This is a very important question to answer for yourself. If you don't have a pool of reserve capital and something major goes wrong with the property, you could find yourself in deep financial trouble. Of all the mistakes that real estate investors make, not having enough reserve capital is probably the most frequent one with the most dire consequences.

As a broker, it's my job to sell real estate. Over the years, I've sold more buildings than I can remember. Most of the investors I have worked with have done well. The ones who haven't succeeded usually got into trouble because they didn't have enough back-up money to cover unexpected expenditures. Two particular investors come to mind. Each of them had a full-time day job and was building a fast portfolio of rental buildings. I remember warning both investors about getting too big too quick with so little money on hand. Neither listened to my advice. In less than three years, both investors had lost all of their buildings and teetered on the verge of bankruptcy. The buildings they owned were good buildings. Instead, inexperience and poor management launched their failure, and the lack of money to bail themselves out was the final blow. Don't let this happen to you. If you commit to long-term investments, be prepared to go the distance and expect the unexpected.

When you decide to attempt long-range ownership, budget all normal expenses, even if you don't think you will be affected by them. For example, factor in the cost of a property management firm even if you plan to manage your own building. Once you dive into your ownership, you might find that the management job is driving you nuts. If you have money built into your budget for a professional manager, you don't have a problem. But if you went skimpy on your numbers because you planned to manage the property yourself, you have troubles.

Also factor into your budget vacancy rates for your property. If the building has not had a vacancy in the last five years, that's great, but don't count on it lasting. Then build in a cost for maintenance and repair. Many lenders use a figure equal to 10 percent of the building's gross rental income to represent this cost. By working up numbers for these types of expenses, you insulate yourself from much of the trouble that pulls other investors down into the financial quicksand.

Before you make a long-term commitment, consider every other issue you can think of, including:

- Will you be able to spend enough time with your family once you have investment properties?
- Does your job allow you enough freedom to be an effective landlord?
- Can you live with your existing car or house until your building matures?

Three-Year Plan

The shortest period of time that I feel you can hold a midterm keeper to reap reasonable profits is three years. Normally, holding buildings longer produces more profits, but you can make good money with investments of short duration. For example, you might buy and restructure an apartment building during your first year of ownership. This might include replacing some tenants, raising rents, reducing operating costs, adding amenities such as additional parking or coin-operated laundries to increase income, and so forth. The second year of ownership should establish a pattern for the profitable changes. By the end of the third year, the building's income may be increased enough to show a good profit as either a building you keep or a building you sell for an adequate profit.

For Example . . .

Assume that recently you purchased a retail space for $350,000. The appreciation rate in the area for this type of building is 3 percent, which holds for all three years you keep the property. By the end of your first year of ownership, the building is worth $360,500. After the second year, it is worth $371,315. And by the time you are ready to sell, the property is worth $382,454. So it appears that you have made $32,454— not a bad profit for three years. However, depending on your costs to purchase, own, and sell the building, your earnings could be much lower. Factor in all expenses when you compute your anticipated profit. ∎

It's difficult to buy a piece of property, hold it for only three years, and turn a decent profit, but it can be done. Buying into a cold market that turns hot is one way to make a short-term investment pay off nicely. Another way is to buy a building and make improvements, either physical or in cash flow. For example, apartment buildings often are valued by the numbers they generate. Appreciation is still a factor, but strong cash flow can increase a building's value quickly, and this is something you might be able to change in a short time. So if you bought a 12-unit apartment building at a low price and re-vamped it to include new tenants, higher rents, and lower expenses, you could conceivably make some money within three years. Physical improvements also could make a property more valuable in a short time.

All in all, I would stay away from a three-year plan. If you want short-term deals, go for quick-flips. The chances of making money are much better when you hold keepers for more than three years.

Five-Year Plan

A five-year deal usually is more viable than a three-year plan; nevertheless, five years still is not a lot of time to build wealth in an average building. To illustrate, let's start with an example.

For Example . . .

Assume that you purchase a duplex for $150,000 and it appreciates at a rate of 5 percent for five years. When you are ready to sell the building after five years, its value is $191,442. If you sell the duplex with a broker's help, you would pay about 7 percent in sales commission, which totals $13,400. (Bro-

kerage commissions are not fixed. They can be any amount a
brokerage and a seller agree on. Because duplexes can be financed as residential property, commissions for selling them
usually are based on residential rates, which can run as low as
5 percent or as high as 7 percent or, really, any amount the two
parties agree on. Larger buildings that are classified as commercial property, such as six-unit apartment buildings, are more
likely to be sold at commercial commission rates, which tend
to be around 10 percent of the sales prices.) This yields gross
profit from the sale of the duplex of $28,042. Of course, you
would have some other expenses in making the sale, and this
profit is based on an assumption that the building has paid for
itself during your ownership. ■

Remember the commercial building in the three-year plan? If
you kept if for five years, the property would have been worth
$405,745. After paying a 10 percent sales commission and recover-
ing your $350,000 purchase price, you would be left with $15,170.
This is certainly much better than the loss of nearly $6,000 when you
kept the property for only three years.

Seven-Year Plan

Keeping a building for seven years gives appreciation time to
work in normal economic markets. It is, however, also a long enough
period of time that significant changes can occur in a property's location. This can be good or bad, depending on the changes. An ownership of seven years also is long enough to expect the possibility of
some major repairs, such as replacement of a furnace or roof. When
you choose a building with an eye toward keeping it, a seven-year
plan usually works well, but you must make sure that the building is
suitable for such a long ownership.

Owning income-producing property for seven years can be a great way to get the most from your investment dollar. True, you do not make money as quickly as you do with quick-flips, but investors often earn handsome profits after fairly long ownerships. Also, it's easier to locate midterm keepers than it is to negotiate quick-flip deals. Sometimes the midterm keepers become retirement properties. The criteria for keeping midterm properties longer include low maintenance cost, good tenants, a stable location, and growing equity.

When an investor sells a building for cash, he must pay considerable taxes. But when equity is allowed to build in a property, the investor's net worth grows without taxation. When the equity is high enough, the investor can borrow against the equity, which gives him ready borrowing power. Most lenders will use equity that exceeds 20 to 30 percent of a property's value as collateral for other purchases. However, some lenders are much more liberal on their loan policies. To determine your borrowing power, talk to several lenders to learn what each of them can do for you. This is a solid plan for expanding and succeeding in real estate.

Evaluating a Midterm Keeper's Potential

When you evaluate a midterm keeper's potential, you must inspect many elements of the property, both physically and on paper. Normally, a licensed building inspector handles the physical inspection. You can do the paper inspection yourself. The following sections look more closely at both types of property evaluations.

Physical Inspections

Physical inspections of real estate are always important; however, most beginning investors are not qualified to perform these inspections effectively. A professional inspection firm can render a lengthy opinion on everything from a building's foundation to the type of paint on the walls. (Buying a building covered in lead paint can be a nightmare.) Don't try to be your own inspector unless you have extensive experience in property inspections and construction methods.

When you look for a building to keep for several years, you want to answer many questions before you buy. For example, how long can you expect the existing roof to last? How old are the heating and cooling systems? Will plumbing need to be replaced in large quantities during your ownership? What are the odds that you will have to repair the parking areas? A professional inspector gives you a long, detailed report on all aspects of a building's physical characteristics. Get this information before you make a final commitment to purchase. You can use a contingency clause in your contract to lock up the property at agreed-upon terms and provide a way out of the deal if the building fails its physical inspection. Chapter 18 goes into great detail on site visits and inspections.

Paper Inspections

Most investors can perform their own paper inspections. In many ways, the paper inspection is more time consuming and difficult than the physical inspection. What are you looking for? As much information as you can find by researching the subject property, neighboring properties, and the surrounding area.

First, dig through all available records on the building you are thinking of buying. For example, if you are evaluating an apartment building, check the property taxes. This information, available at the tax assessor's office, is open for public inspection. What are current and past rents? What is the cost of landlord utilities? The listing broker or the seller should be able to provide answers to these questions. How much money has been spent on maintenance and repairs in the last ten years? Again, the listing broker or seller should be able to document these costs. What vacancy rate has the building experi-enced in the last ten years? For this information, review the financial records on the building that the seller provides. Find out all you can about the subject property, then move on to other investigations.

Your next step is to look into neighboring properties. Deter-mine their sales prices, vacancy rates, rents, and maintenance costs by talking with real estate brokers. Learn as much as you can about your competitors.

Now evaluate the neighborhood. Consult past police reports for the area to assess the crime rate. Scan old newspapers at the library or talk to local law enforcement officers for an overview of the crime activity in the area. (Information of this type can be difficult to ob-tain from big-city police departments; they simply don't have the time to devote to personal requests.) Evaluate the area to see whether it is growing, stable, or declining. Obviously, properties in growing communities offer the most potential, and real estate in declining neighborhoods comes cheap for a reason. Study old newspapers to assess how long it takes landlords to rent apartments in the area. You can do this by tracking the classified advertisements and noticing how long ads with the same addresses and phone numbers ran before they were stopped.

Finally, talk to the tenants in the building you want to buy. Most landlords will not object to you doing so unless they have some-thing to hide. If you can, also talk to tenants in neighboring build-ings. The more effort you put into your investigation, the less likely you are to get stuck with a building you will not want to keep.

CHAPTER 6

Buy It—Retire with It

At what age would you like to retire? Retirement means different things to different people. Some see retirement as a curse, while others see it as an opportunity to enjoy life more. No law says you must retire when you turn 65. No law says you can't retire at age 45. If you support yourself without working, consider yourself retired. Many retired people do work, however. They quit one career to work at something else, either to make ends meet or to remain active. Real estate is an excellent vehicle for retirement. If you invest wisely, you can retire early, enjoy a good annual income, and participate as little or as much as you like in your investment portfolio.

Some people find themselves troubled financially when retirement time comes. Real estate is a viable solution to the problems some people face when they must retire. If an investor starts early enough, it's possible to build a mighty empire of real estate that can be a money machine when it's time to retire. No magic is involved in real estate, just sound business principles. Some of these principles are examined in the following sections.

Why Invest in Keepers?

Buildings that fit the profile of excellent retirement investments are what I call keepers; that is, the real estate will be held for many years, not sold for a quick profit. When you decide to build a real estate portfolio that will take care of you financially in later life, you are making a long-term commitment. It may not be possible to sell buildings that are great for retirement purposes for a quick profit. This is okay if your plan to keep them remains in effect, but you must be fairly sure of yourself before you buy keepers because getting rid of them without losing money can be a problem.

Investors often buy properties as keepers even when the buildings will not pay for themselves entirely when they are purchased. The same investors probably never would consider buying a midterm keeper that would not pay for itself. Then why are they willing to take keepers that produce negative cash flows? The investors are motivated by their intent to have the buildings pay off over a longer period of time. Because keepers can cost money to hold and operate, it's common for investors who own them to deal in quick-flips and midterm keepers as well. The cash flows from these other investments help pay for the keepers until they can pay for themselves. Holding a mixed bag of property can be a good way to enjoy all the benefits available from various types of real estate.

How to Recognize a Keeper

Learning to identify a potentially profitable keeper probably will take some time if you are new to the real estate game. Some buildings that look like keepers are not, while others that don't appear to be good investments can be. You can't judge a property by its profit-and-loss statement alone. It's not unusual for a keeper to operate in the red. If the negative cash flow is not too severe, the loss shown annually doesn't have to rule out the building. You must look at all angles of a property when you plan to retire with it in your portfolio. It's certain that you will have expenses with buildings you keep for a long time, and this is also something you must consider.

Because investors will hold their keepers for a long time, the buildings must possess certain qualities. A property's potential is the first element to consider when looking for a keeper. You must evaluate present conditions, but future possibilities are also important in retirement properties. Let's say, for example, that you are considering the purchase of an apartment building whose heating system consists of a huge steam boiler and old radiators. This might not concern you if you were looking at the building as a quick-flip. Neither might the outdated heating system bother you if your plan was to sell the building in five years. But an antique heating system in a building that you will keep for decades should be a red flag of financial danger. You know that eventually you will have to replace the heating mechanisms. Estimates from heating contractors indicate that the cost of converting the old steam system to a modern setup will be steep. Maybe you should pass on the property and opt for a more modern building. Either way, steam heat is a good example of one potential problem to look out for.

A building's roof also could present some problems. For example, a slate roof is durable and can last for a long time. However, repairs to slate roofs are expensive, and replacing them with asphalt shingles can be extremely costly, due to the removal of the slate. Also, a building with a flat roof likely will give a landlord more trouble than a building with a pitched roof. Buildings without gutters or other storm water drainage facilities may have leaking or damaged foundations. While many construction features don't affect a building's short-term ownership, the same issues can be major problems for long-term investors.

Construction details are not the only things to consider when shopping for keepers. Check a building's history before you invest.

Has it had good tenants? Was the vacancy rate high in the last ten years? Does the building house subsidized tenants? Does it meet the criteria to house subsidized tenants, or will it need improvements to meet those standards if you choose to run a subsidized building? Who has managed the property over the last several years? If you find that a landlord has gone through a long list of management companies, investigate the reasons for the turnover; it could indicate a problem building. Check old tax records to determine whether the building's value has escalated in recent years. Run a check on comparable buildings that have sold over the last five years. Compare the sales information to determine whether values in the area have appreciated regularly. Dig deep and find out all you can to help you evaluate the building for stability and growth.

Not all of your evaluations will be based on fact. For example, you need a good feeling for a property if you plan to retire with it. Are you comfortable with the building type and design? Do you like its location? Can you envision how you will make the property more valuable over time? Also, what is the location like in terms of stability, growth, crime, and so forth? After many years in the business, you will develop reliable gut reactions to buildings you evaluate. Finding your first good keepers may be exciting, frustrating, fun, or a little of each. After awhile, the work of recognizing and investigating a keeper becomes routine. What may seem like an endless chore on your first few properties soon evolves into a methodical approach to securing your retirement, and you probably will learn to enjoy the results—and possibly the work itself.

Finding Hidden Treasure

Who hasn't dreamed of finding hidden treasure? I enjoy treasure hunting with a metal detector, but I don't really expect to find a buried chest full of gold. However, when I search for real estate to buy, I know that I can find buildings with the potential to become treasure troves. None of my properties has ever made me rich beyond my wildest dreams, but I have made a good living and a lot of money with real estate. You can, too, once you know what to look for and what to do with it when you find it.

Some people uncover real treasure in the walls, attics, and basements of buildings. But for the real estate investor, the treasure she seeks is not gold and silver bars. Astute investors pursue much larger treasure that continues to pay off year after year after year. The treasure they seek is the building itself. Sometimes investors find buildings already in their treasure states. By this, I mean that the buildings are good investments just as they are. In most cases, however, buildings need to be primed to become cash producers. If a building is already a good investment, it is unlikely that the owner will be interested in selling it, except under certain circumstances. It is the building that offers the *potential* for wealth that you can take advantage of. Let's look at an example.

For Example . . .

Let's say that an elderly couple own and reside in a large Victorian home. People have tried to buy the home off and on over the 35 years they have lived there, but the couple will not sell. Recent changes in the zoning laws allow houses in the area, like this one, to be used for professional space. If you could buy the house, you could convert it to offices for dentists, lawyers, accountants, and other professionals. The income potential would be terrific, but the couple don't want to move out of their home. You and other investors see the profit potential, but no one has found the map to the treasure yet. With a little creative thinking, you come up with a plan that just might help you acquire the house and accommodate the couple's wishes.

You learn that the elderly couple are getting by financially, but don't have much money left over after paying their bills—a stressful situation. Their savings account is small, and the house is all they have that is worth much. Because they don't want to move, they are unwilling to sell the house. You see owning the property as a tremendous money-making opportunity; however, you understand the couple's concerns due to their advanced age and declining health. Therefore, you offer to buy the house at a fair market value. You agree to give them a life estate in the home which means that they will pay you rent out of the money they get from the sale in exchange for the ability to live in the house for the rest of their lives or until they require an adult-care facility.

The couple accept your offer, and everyone wins. You get the house before any other investor. The couple continue to live in their own home and enjoy a large sum of money in their savings account. Rent paid to you covers most of the mortgage costs and comes out of the sale proceeds so the couple are not strapped for cash. You also should see some tax benefits from the deal, and you will enjoy property appreciations. Once the house is vacant, you can convert it and make the big money you anticipate. A deal like this, that benefits everyone involved, is not difficult to accomplish if you remain flexible and open-minded. In this example, while all the other investors offered only straight sales, you won the keeper by using a patient, winning plan. ■

Negotiating the Purchase of Prime Properties

Negotiating and planning the purchase of prime properties is a big part of making it big as a real estate investor. You've just seen an example of how these skills can turn an unapproachable deal into a solid purchase. If you want something badly enough, you usually can find a way to get it. This is not to say that you can have everything you want or that anyone will sell anything under the right terms. But on plenty of occasions, using skills you've built in negotiating and planning results in success. Begin by reading some of the many books written on the subject of negotiating. Study them closely. Learn from them. Practice what you've learned by staging mock negotiating events with friends and family members. Negotiating skills will help you in many aspects of life, as well as enhance your real estate career.

To be a good negotiator, you need to know what you have to offer the person on the other side of the bargaining table. In the earlier example about the elderly couple, you would have had little room to work if you did not know about life estates. A reverse mortgage also might have worked in the situation. You must prepare yourself well for all aspects of your new business, as you are doing by reading this book. Think of it as earning your investor's degree. Anyone with money who is of legal age and competence can buy real estate. This is not to say that anyone can be a successful real estate investor. Most people can become profitable investors, but the returns don't always come easily. You need to work and study to reach your maximum potential.

You can use negotiating skills to settle everything from disputes over who will pay the points at closing to how much a seller will lower a sales price in view of construction defects uncovered during an inspection. Before you start negotiating, however, you need a written plan. Once you find a building you want to buy, determine how you will negotiate its purchase. It is standard procedure for most real estate negotiations to take place in writing, in the form of an offer to purchase. This is good because it means you don't have to make snap decisions and talk off the top of your head. You can formulate a good offer and present it. If it comes back with a counteroffer, you can take time to work out your next offer or decide whether to accept the counteroffer.

An experienced buyer's broker can be a lot of help to you during this phase of your work. I strongly recommend that most investors find and engage buyers' brokers to help them develop their rental portfolio. Look for a broker who specializes in the type of property you are interested in buying. Chapter 16 covers this issue in more detail.

Take Baby Steps When Buying Keepers

Never jump into the purchase of real estate keepers all at one time. You are more likely to be successful if you build this part of your rental portfolio by taking your time and investing wisely. The best buildings are not always available when you want to buy them. This requires you to be patient as you wait for the right properties to come along. Diving into the keeper market with a wide-open checkbook could be disastrous. Because keepers are not always cash producers when you buy them, their negative cash flow could drain your reserve capital and force you out of the real estate game. It is far better, for most people, to buy keepers at a steady pace rather than acquiring several at one time.

On many occasions, you may have an opportunity to buy more than one property from a single seller at reduced prices. Sometimes these deals can be extremely profitable, but they also can spell trouble for investors who don't have substantial financial backing. I've often listed several properties at a time for an individual seller. In most cases, the seller is willing to take a lower price for his buildings if all of the buildings are sold as a package deal. The catch can be, however, that one or more of the buildings are below par or do not fit the buyer's game plan. As they say, a bad bargain at any price is still a bad bargain. You might like the idea of buying in bulk to get a reduced price, but what you save at the time of the purchase could bring you undue hardship later. For example, if you want to buy keepers, but wind up with quick-flips in the package, you might suffer financial hardship. However, if you wish to build a mixed portfolio, bulk sales are well worth considering. It's rare that all buildings in a sales package are suitable keepers.

I recommend buying keepers at a slow pace, but the term means different things to different investors. For some, it's buying one building every two months. Other investors think a slow pace is buying one building each year. The time spread varies from person to person. However, one thing is true universally: if you buy too many potential keepers at a time and later find that they are not of keeper quality, you could get into deep financial difficulty. Pick a pace that is right for you and move forward, but don't overextend yourself in the process.

Owning a nice assortment of keeper real estate can make your real estate career—and possibly your life—happier. Pride of ownership is one benefit. Growing your rental portfolio to a point where it produces adequate income for you to quit your job also could be quite rewarding. Retiring with the comfort of a sizable income and a great deal of equity in real estate should make anyone happier. Although money doesn't buy happiness, it sure can help to make so much of life more enjoyable. Invest wisely in the proper real estate, and you have a tremendous opportunity to be both happy and self-sufficient as your real estate holdings grow.

CHAPTER 7

You Can Invest on a Shoestring

Can you really buy real estate without a lot of cash for a down payment?

Absolutely. The exact amount of money you need to start buying investment real estate varies, depending on lenders, buyers, sellers, property types, and other variables. You will need some cash or equity to pledge, however. (Investors sometimes leave their closings with more money than they had when they bought their buildings. This money is not profit, though; it is leveraged money. This means it must be paid back at some point, but in the meantime it creates cash flow.) Even if the cash never leaves your bank account, it needs to be there. So how much do you really need? It depends on what you are buying and how you are acquiring the property. Because property values cover a broad range, it's impossible to pinpoint a figure. Plus, the financing terms have a lot to do with the amount of money needed. Depending on property values in your area and your negotiating abilities, however, you likely can get into the game with less than $10,000—and you might not even need that much.

Back in the 1980s, a lot of investors flocked to no-money-down deals. As a seller of real estate, I offered my buyers a number of incentives that reduced their need for out-of-pocket cash. Some of the deals that I did in the 1980s would be financial suicide today. Tax law changes in 1986 and inflation have made highly leveraged real estate a ticking time bomb. You still can buy real estate with small amounts of cash, but the game has changed over the years.

The amount of money you need to get into real estate ownership depends on the types of loans you qualify for and the types of property you wish to buy. For example, if your military service makes you eligible for a VA loan and you wish to buy a rental property that contains four or fewer units, one of which you will live in, your down payment could be nearly nonexistent and the seller would have to pay the points to close the loan. If you don't have VA eligibility, a Federal Housing Administration (FHA) loan would require you to pay less than 5 percent of the purchase price as a down payment. For a conventional loan, the minimum down payment usually is about 5 percent of the purchase price. Some of the down payment and closing costs can come as a gift from parents or relatives. Creative financing is not dead, but the rules for success have changed.

No Money Down: An Investor's Dream

Investors often dream of no-money-down deals. Even in today's market, such deals do exist and investors find them. But their risk tends to be higher than it used to be. When real estate appreciated by leaps and bounds, year after year, investors could enter into highly leveraged deals and still come out winners. The same deals in a stable or sluggish economy rarely work. Based on recent real estate activity, no-money-down deals usually are not worth the risk in the current market.

If you buy a property without sinking any money into the investment, you generally have no equity. In some markets, a building could lose value and you would find yourself owing more than the building is worth. At the least, you would not gain appreciation or equity. Whenever you have little to no equity in real estate, your risk is great. Unless you can afford to lose money, you probably should ignore the temptation of no-money-down deals.

When a seller offers a proposition that does not require a buyer to come up with cash, it's usually because the seller needs the sale desperately. The offer of a no-money-down deal should put you on red alert for danger. Sometimes offers are made due to divorce or other personal problems and can be good opportunities. More often, however, the chance to buy property without a down payment means that you are either paying too much for the property or buying something that other people are not interested in owning.

There is a difference between a seller offering you full financing and you arranging it yourself. You can buy property without using your cash when you pledge your money or equity in other assets as collateral for a loan. When sellers offer to provide you with financing themselves, be careful. The deals can be quite tempting, but they can be just as dangerous. Owner financing—or seller financing, whatever you want to call it—can become one of your worst nightmares.

Sellers who finance their own sales might slant the loan contracts heavily in their favor. You may not get the same protection that you would when you secure financing from a commercial lender. In some cases, you might make major improvements to a property, fall onto hard times, miss a few payments, and lose your investment to the person who sold you the building and financed the loan.

Another risk of owner financing is that most lenders do not allow an owner who owes money on a property to offer full seller financing. Older loans don't always have acceleration clauses, but newer loans usually do. A loan that has an acceleration clause gives the lender the right to demand that the buyer pay off the loan in full if the seller transfers the property with an installment contract. In other words, the loan is not necessarily assumable, and if the lender doesn't approve of an assumption when an acceleration clause exists, it can demand payment in full. If payment is not made, the lender has the right to foreclose on the property. If a seller owes a bank money on a building and arranges a private sale and financing with you while the building remains financed at the bank in the seller's name, you could be in for severe trouble. You might make all of your payments regularly to the seller and still lose the property because the seller might not pay the bank's mortgage. In this case, the bank would have a right to foreclose on the property. The whole thing can get very nasty. Therefore, if you have any inclination to participate in seller financing, I strongly suggest that you run every document past an excellent real estate attorney before signing anything.

Using Money without Spending It

If you have equity in real estate, money in certificates of deposit, or other assets, you can use your equity, cash, or assets as security for a loan without actually surrendering them. This can be very important when withdrawing money could trigger tax consequences that would cause you to lose a portion of your cash to the IRS. Many retirement investments, such as individual retirement accounts, are tax deferred. If you take money out of an account before the full term of the investment instrument has expired, you probably will have to pay taxes on the money at your present tax level. But if you do not withdraw the money you use as collateral, it should not trigger the tax axe. I am not a tax expert, however, and you should consult a tax professional before making any major financial decisions.

You can use many assets for leverage, depending on the lender with which you work. Some examples of assets that might be substituted for cash follow:

- Individual retirement accounts
- Bonds
- Mutual funds

- Annual annuities
- Employee pension funds
- Stocks
- Equity in other real estate
- Trust funds
- Equity in a business
- Contractual agreements
- Alimony
- Certificates of deposit
- Cash in money market accounts
- Coin collections
- Anything of value a lender will accept

Avoiding potential taxes is only one reason for using leverage. Another advantage is that your money remains in its current investment, earning even more for you. While your assets are leveraged as collateral, you will not be able to access the money and spend it, but they act as an equity position in the real estate you purchase, which enhances your financial safety. Once you obtain and hold enough real estate, you should be able to use the equity in your buildings to continue expanding your portfolio without having to dip into your cash on hand.

When you use equity in one building as a down payment for another building, the lender generally places a mortgage on the first building, as well as on the new building. If the down payment comes from a cash investment you are pledging, the lender places a lien against the cash investment. The lender is protected nicely, and you benefit because you don't have to withdraw your cash.

Making a Low Down Payment

A low down payment, say 5 percent of the purchase price, can be both good and bad—good because you need little money up front, but bad because of the reasons cited earlier when we discussed no-money-down deals. You have a few ways to keep down payment requirements low. One of the easiest ways is to buy a small apartment building—one with four or fewer dwelling units—and live in one of the apartments as your primary residence. This can keep a down payment at or below 5 percent of the purchase price. You don't have to live in the building forever. You can stay for a month or so, then decide to buy another apartment building. When you buy the new property, it becomes your home and the first one is your investment. This system works very well for some investors who are just starting out.

If you do not buy property that is suitable as a primary residence, you must look to other means for acquiring the real estate with little cash. Seller financing for part of the loan amount can be used quite effectively, for instance. (We will talk more about this option later in the chapter.) Buying property well below its appraised value also can open the door to a low down payment. Sometimes a lender bases its loans on a percentage of appraised value and doesn't require the investor to come up with a portion of the sales price if she is purchasing the property far enough below the appraised value to meet the loan-to-value ratios the lender sets. This type of arrangement is difficult to find, but it is a possibility.

Appraised value represents the maximum figure a lender will consider when determining a down payment. But no law requires a buyer to pay appraised value. Many times, sellers accept less than full appraised value. Conditions that might influence a seller to take less than the appraised value include the following:

- Divorce
- Relocation
- Desire to change investment types
- Loss of income
- Breakup of a partnership
- Damaged property

- Illness
- Increased time demands
- Any circumstance that warrants a quick sale

Down payment requirements and strategies vary depending on lenders, buyers, sellers, and other factors. The type of property you buy also can influence the down payment amount. For example, it's common for owner-occupied buildings to require a minimum down payment of 5 percent while the same nonowner-occupied property would require a minimum of 20 percent, or more.

When an Owner Finances the Sale

Getting an owner to finance a sale, or a portion of a sale, can be wonderful. I've already told you that it also can be dangerous because the legal agreements often are biased, and the buyer may have little equity in the property being purchased. If you are willing to gamble on the equity, a good attorney can help you overcome the legal issues. Finding a seller who is willing to participate in some aspect of the financing is especially handy when buying commercial property and large multifamily buildings.

If you arrange a deal solely with the owner of a property and never meet with a broker or a banker, make sure you have a good lawyer looking after your best interests. Not all sellers who finance their own sales are looking to take advantage of you. Many sellers prefer to receive their money a little at a time to reduce their tax liabilities. I presently am buying some land with full owner financing, and the elderly seller doesn't want me to pay off the loan all at once. He owns extensive real estate and is not interested in quick cash that would be hit hard by taxes. A lawyer I know looks at his land sales the same way.

When you find a seller who is willing to finance a portion of a sale, you may be on the verge of a great opportunity. However, the attractive financing should not be what pushes you to make a purchasing decision. Decide whether you would buy the building if the financing were not so attractive. If you feel the property is a good deal with or without seller financing, proceed in your purchase arrangements. But if you realize that your main motivation for the purchase is the financing, walk away. Many purchase and financing agreements require little money and even invite tarnished credit; however, you must enter such deals with extreme caution.

Leaving the Closing with Money in Your Pocket

When a seller helps you finance a commercial building, which includes an apartment building with five or more units, you can leave the closing table with more money in your pocket than you entered the room with. It may seem strange to think of buying a building for $250,000 and completing the transaction with money in your pocket, but I've arranged many deals where investors basically have been paid to buy apartment buildings.

If no-money-down deals are dangerous—and they can be—then a deal in which you borrow more money than a building costs must be extremely perilous. Yes, it's true that it's a high-risk investment, but it can turn out to be very profitable if you have the nerves of steel it takes to enter into the arena of over-leveraged properties. Plus, you need a very liberal lender unless you get full seller financing. Even with all the hazards, though, the reward can outweigh the risk. However, the decision to enter into this type of deal must be an individual one.

To walk away from a closing with new money in your pocket, you must buy a building for less than it is worth and convince the seller to participate in the financing. To illustrate this, let me give you a brief history of an actual deal.

For Example . . .

I had an investor who wanted to buy a 12-unit apartment building. The property was worth $250,000, but the owner was willing to sell it for $230,000. My investor was a 30-year-old welder who dreamed of becoming a landlord. The seller was an older man who dreamed of ending his career as a landlord. The investor offered the seller $250,000 for the building, subject to the seller working with him on the financing. Because the seller was willing to take $230,000 for the building, he accepted the deal. My investor got a bank loan for 80 percent of the sales price or the appraised value, whichever was lower. In this case, the figures were the same, and the investor got loan approval from the bank for $200,000. The seller held a second mortgage for the balance of the sales price and the closing costs, and paid the buyer at the table for the difference. In short, the investor got the building for appraised value, used none of his money, and essentially received a seven-year loan from the seller to help turn the building around and make it a cash producer. These deals don't happen often, and they require skillful manipulation, but they can be done. ■

Forming Partnerships to Conserve Capital

Partnerships in real estate can propel investors to new heights quickly. They allow entrepreneurs to pool their money and talents to capitalize on the real estate market. Partnerships also can be the undoing of otherwise successful investors. Many types of partnerships exist. You might consider a money-money partnership to conserve your capital. In this situation, you and another person each cover one-half of all expenses (assuming we are talking about a 50-50 partnership). Another type of partnership might require you to put up money while your partner offers special skills or labor, such as remodeling work. A partnership can consist of as few as two people or as many people as you want to let in on your deal. Usually, smaller partnerships work best.

My first venture with a partner, a certified public accountant, worked out well. He put up the money, and I put up the expertise for rehab work. Together we bought rundown houses, fixed them up, then flipped them quickly for a profit. The deals worked well, and the returns were lucrative. We enjoyed a strong partnership for a couple of years. The point is, if you have special skills to offer but little money, you, too, can work with a partner who will use her credit and cash so that you both come out winners.

You also could join forces with a friend or two to buy a large property or a long-term investment. Personally, I would stay away from partnership deals to invest in property you plan to hold for a long time. Getting out without financial loss can be very difficult. Once you sign a mortgage note for a loan on a property with another person, you are committed for the length of the loan. It's rare that a lender will do a novation (release one party from the loan), even in the case of divorce. You could be stuck with your partner for 30 years with some loans, so don't enter a long-term deal without giving it a lot of thought or without getting the proper legal advice from an attorney. I favor using partnerships for quick-flips, but partners can benefit you in any real estate venture.

Not all partnerships are equal. For example, you might provide money or a service that is valued at 35 percent of the total deal. This would give your partner 65 percent of the deal. As a general partner, you can be held financially accountable for your partners' actions. In a limited partnership, however, the most you can lose is the amount you invest in the partnership. Always talk with at least one lawyer and several tax professionals before you enter into any type of partnership.

Highly Leveraged Deals

Highly leveraged deals have the potential to be bank account busters. Be wary of them, and set up some safeguards for yourself if you roll the dice in high-risk deals. The best protection is to have plenty of money to keep yourself out of trouble. Unfortunately, average investors don't have a lot of cash lying around. If you tie all of your real estate together with equity loans, the loss of one property could cause you to lose others. If your business is not protected under a corporate structure, your personal finances and home also could be at risk. Even with a corporate umbrella, you may find yourself attacked on a personal level. Again, consult with good attorneys to protect yourself in all the ways possible.

Simple ways to reduce your risk exist. Start by maintaining an adequate amount of reserve capital for unexpected needs. Establish a line of credit for building maintenance and repair so you are not scrambling for a loan when a heating system must be replaced. Consider establishing a corporate structure for your real estate holdings. Don't sign any documents you don't understand completely. Build a relationship with at least one lawyer and one tax expert. Most importantly, don't get greedy. If you play your cards right, you can win more than you lose in real estate, but make darn sure you can afford the losses that are sure to accompany the wins.

CHAPTER 8

Investing in Detached Single-Family Homes

Single-family homes are a big part of the American dream for most people. In fact, plenty of people do anything they can to own their own homes. In terms of being places to live, houses are ideal for most of the population. However, detached single-family homes are not a prime investment for most real estate entrepreneurs who do not plan to reside in the dwellings. Generally speaking, houses do not provide positive cash flow. Small apartment buildings typically generate much better numbers than detached homes do. Yet some investors, like myself, do well with houses in their investment portfolios. The great thing about real estate is that very few rules apply to all investors. This gives everyone a chance to seek his own level, which broadens the spectrum of the playing field for investors.

Most people who buy buildings for their first real estate ventures buy single-family homes. They might buy houses, townhouses, condos, or co-ops, but most investors buy places to live that don't involve managing tenants. Other people buy duplexes or larger apartment buildings to live in and manage.

Once people own houses to live in, they sometimes consider buying other houses as investments. Often, however, they buy the other houses for their own residences and turn their previous homes into rental property. This might be the case when a person buys a condo as a first purchase, then buys and moves into a detached home. Regardless of the motivation, single-family homes can be rented quickly in most markets, but the rental rates may not cover the cost of owning the property. This is considered a negative cash flow and is not the ideal situation for an investor. However, houses can be considered keepers when investors don't require positive cash flow at the time of purchase.

Houses Can Be Great Places to Live

Houses offer shelter, privacy, comfort and often tax advantages. Given an opportunity to either rent or own a house, most people would choose ownership. Single-family homes don't always work out as investments for a number of reasons. First, it's difficult to rent houses at prices that produce positive cash flow. When the only investment you have is a vacant rental house, you must continue to pay the mortgage even if the property currently is not producing income. If tenants come and go frequently so that you must rerent the house each year, the refurbishing expenses can destroy any profit that might have been possible. In general, houses generate big expenses for little potential income.

If houses are such terrible investments, why do so many investors own them? Houses are not bad investments; they simply are not the best investments for most people. A majority of real estate entrepreneurs don't have the time or the skills needed to make single-family homes pay off as investments. Investors who do have the time and skills can see solid financial rewards. Also, investors who buy keepers can buy houses, then sit on them for a few years until the numbers indicate positive cash flow. If you are looking for a good investment that will produce money soon, however, a house probably isn't it unless you have experience in remodeling or contracting work.

Advantages to Buying Single-Family Homes

Most real estate investors agree that although single-family homes don't provide superior income opportunities for average investors, they do offer some advantages. For example, houses can be much easier to sell than apartment buildings, shopping centers, retail stores, and office space. If an investor needs to liquidate, houses can be one of the easiest types of real estate to sell in a hurry because most housebuyers are consumers rather than investors. Another advantage to homes is their price in relationship to that of apartment buildings and commercial property. It can take a lot less money to buy a house than it might to buy other types of real estate.

Patient investors can purchase a house each year to move up the portfolio ladder. For example, you might buy a house this year to live in. (Down payment requirements for owner-occupied homes often are very low.) Then, after living in the home for a year, you might rent it to a tenant and buy another house to live in. Because you live in each house you buy, your down payment is lower than it would be for an investor. If you started this process when you were 25 years old and stopped it when you retired at age 65, you would own 40 houses to support you in your retirement years. Some of the houses would be paid for, others would be partially paid for, and your rental income would be on track with the rate of inflation. This is not a bad plan. If you can act as a general contractor and build yourself a new house each year, as I have done in the past, the profits are even sweeter.

When you buy single-family homes, you have the ability to mix the locations of your rental property, which can be an advantage. If you buy a 12-unit apartment building, all of your apartments in the building are basically in the same location. Therefore, a mistake in judging the property's location could devastate you financially. If you buy 12 houses in 12 different areas, however, one mistake in judgment will not drag you down. It's like the law of physics: for every action, an equal but opposite reaction occurs. This concept applies, to some extent, to how investors find their own niches in the real estate market.

Houses Can Generate Negative Cash Flow

Negative cash flow is common with houses used for rental property. Of course, not all houses experience cash losses. Some can be rented for enough to pay all the expenses of owning and operating the houses as rental properties. When negative cash flow occurs, investors must be willing to subsidize their investments until inflation and appreciation allow the income to swing in a positive direction. It's possible to find a house that you can buy and rent immediately, and experience a positive cash flow. Part of the puzzle is the amount of cash you apply to the purchase of the home. Other factors include market rents, management costs, and necessary improvements.

Should you buy a single-family home even when you believe it will generate financial losses during the year? It depends on your financial strength and your future plans as an investor. A lot of people try to invest in properties that will pay for themselves from the first day of ownership. The burden of buying such properties is a heavy one. Sometimes you can be better off in the long run by purchasing a house that will not make money right away. However, you must be prepared to shell out cash each month to keep the property viable until conditions change and create a positive cash flow.

For Example . . .

Let's say that you find a nice house in a great location and want to buy it. The home is valued at $150,000. Based on your calculations, the home would be rented quickly, but the expected rent would fall short of paying all ownership expenses by about $200 each month. In your first year of ownership, this amounts to $2,400. Plus, if the tenant moves, you may have to repaint the home's interior. All in all, you guess that you will spend about $3,300 in addition to your investment income to keep up the house for a year. The local appreciation rate has run about 4 percent for the last three years. You expect the value of the house to increase by 4 percent in your first year of ownership. If it does, the property will be worth $156,000 by the end of the year. This would give you a paper profit of $2,700 at year end. The money would not be accessible unless you sold the house, and the cost of selling it would eat up the small profit. In your second year, however, you assume that you could increase the rental fee and that the house would continue to appreciate—another paper profit. However, you must spend some money to keep the house going. So is this a wise investment? ■

Investors with deep pockets would have no problem with a deal like the one described above. They can afford to take cash losses for awhile as long as their investments build equity and eventually yield cash profits. The investors earn paper profits, and the cash outlay is not too high. Other investors would struggle to make ends meet on the deal, and any unexpected problems, such as the need to evict a tenant or install a new heating system, could crush them financially. You must decide for yourself whether you can handle the risk of negative cash flow. Will your potential for loss ruin your investment career? If so, don't take the gamble. If you keep the house long enough, it should pay off, but you will skate on thin ice for a few years. Therefore, you must maintain enough cash or credit to keep yourself out of trouble. Negative cash flow is something most investors don't want, but many investors accept it under certain conditions.

Establishing Rent-to-Buy Programs

One way to collect rent on a house that is higher than the market rent is to offer a rent-to-buy program. This system can work extremely well. Before the tax laws changed, I was building about 60 houses a year. Of those homes, about half of them served as rental property. Although it's somewhat rare to build new houses for rental property, I had a plan that worked well. The new homes were available for sale, but also were offered as rent-to-buy properties so that the partnership that I was involved in received some good tax advantages. I authorized the people working for me as property managers to allow pets in the homes, but with a higher rental rate to offset the possible damage to the houses. A straight rental of a new home was sometimes allowed, but most of the houses were filled with people who rented them with the intent of purchasing the homes. A portion of their inflated rent was to be applied to a purchaser's closing costs when a sale was completed. This simple system increased the rent I could collect by about 25 percent. At that time, houses in the area were renting for about $500 a month. My houses rented for $625 a month.

My rent-to-buy program worked for several reasons. The most obvious was the much higher rental income I received. I also attracted better tenants who took care of the homes because they intended to buy them. The lack of turnover in tenants saved me money, too. When people bought the homes, I applied some of their rent to their closing costs. This was not a loss because I made money on the sale. Many people never saved enough money for down payments, so they continued on the rent-to-buy program. This gave me tax advantages and increased income, as well as good tenants.

You probably will not build new houses to rent out, but you still can benefit from the rent-to-buy program. If you purchase a property and rent it in a manner similar to what I have described, you can turn a house that may have produced a negative cash flow into a winner. Most tenants will pay extra if you allow them to keep pets. Many people are interested in rent-to-buy programs. You can build rental rate increases into the option you sign with a tenant to buy your home. The sales price of the home can be locked in or left floating, based on a current appraisal at the time of sale. Apply any money you credit back to the tenant to the closing costs, not the down payment, assuming you seek the rental income and don't really want to sell the house in a hurry. This gives the tenant a fair deal financially, but can slow down the deal's pace as the tenant saves for the needed down payment. As with most aspects of real estate, consult with an attorney before you engage in a rent-to-buy program. Also have your attorney draft the agreements for rent-to-buy deals.

Pros and Cons of Managing Detached Homes

Managing detached homes can be a hassle if you own many of them. If you own an apartment building with six units, you can manage all of the dwellings by visiting a single location. When you own six detached homes, they probably are not in the same neighborhood. While it's wise to invest in several locations, it does require more effort when managing multiple properties. Driving all over town to show properties to prospective tenants or to collect rent is more trouble than going to a single building.

Driving is not the only potential drawback to owning detached homes. If you own a four-unit apartment building, the building may operate on a single heating system. In the case of detached homes, each needs its own heating system. One well or water connection can service a four-unit building, but four wells or water connections are required for four detached homes. You see the pattern here. Because they are independent structures, houses require one of everything, while apartment buildings don't. This makes the cost of buying and operating detached homes potentially more expensive.

When you use a single-family home to generate rental income and the house goes vacant, your income stops. When you rent out a duplex, a vacancy in one unit cuts your rental income in half, but half is better than none. The higher cost of renting a single-family home can make a house more difficult to lease than an apartment. On the other hand, many people prefer to live in houses, so a house might rent much faster, and you might get a more stable tenant.

If you are forced to put a new roof on a house, you incur considerable expense for a single rental unit. Reroofing a four-unit building might cost a little more, but you would have four rental units to return the cost instead of one. Repairs and maintenance are both considerations when deciding between houses and apartment buildings.

General management of detached homes can be quite easy. If you draft your rental agreements properly and find good tenants, you have little more to do than retrieve your rent from the mailbox each month. In many ways, houses are easier to manage than apartments. People who rent houses tend to be more settled. They often stay for several years before moving. This cuts down on a landlord's expenses and increases profits. On the other hand, it's safe to expect a high turnover rate with tenants who live in one-bedroom apartments. Houses definitely have their place in an investor's rental portfolio.

Use Your Own Home as a Springboard to Success

Using the equity in your own home to help you buy other properties is one way to launch your real estate career quickly. Of course this move is risky. If the properties you buy with leverage from your home go sour, you could lose your home as well as the other properties. Therefore, before you put your home equity on the line, you must be comfortable that you are making a safe and wise decision.

You have two basic ways to use the equity in your home to buy other properties. You could get a second mortgage on your house and receive a cash loan to start your investing career. Or you could pledge the equity in your home as a down payment for another property. Either way, if the new property fails, your home is at great risk. Talk to some local experts, like lawyers and accountants, before you use the equity in your home to buy other buildings. The decision to gamble your home is one that only you can make. Generally speaking, professional investors hesitate to gamble their own homes, but anxious investors who need grub stakes may take the risk. My best advice is to look for another source of funding, but use your home equity if you are willing to take a chance on losing.

Depending on where you live, you may consider the purchase of a condo or a co-op for rental income. Some aspects of these purchases are similar to those of detached housing. However, several key differences exist. For example, when you buy a co-op apartment, you are not buying real estate at all; you are buying stock in a corporation that owns the apartment building. To learn about condos and co-ops as investments, let's move to the next chapter.

CHAPTER 9

Condos and Co-ops as Investment Property

Condominiums (condos) and cooperatives (co-ops) are prevalent is some areas and rare in others, although condos are much more abundant than co-ops. Both types of dwellings can be similar in appearance, but differences exist, as well. Co-ops are most often apartments that are not used as conventional apartments. A corporation is formed to either build or buy an apartment building. Co-op owners are sold stock in the corporation that allows them to live in one of the apartments. The buyers of co-ops *do not*—I repeat—*do not* own real estate; they own stock in a corporation. When a buyer purchases a condo, she owns the property interior, but not the exterior or the grounds. These are very different types of ownership than traditional homeowners are accustomed to.

Across the United States, condos are popular investment properties. Many investors buy condos at beaches or ski resorts. Co-ops, generally associated with large cities, usually are not considered to be as glamorous as condos. Of course, there are exceptions to most rules, and some co-op buildings are very prestigious. From an investor's point of view, condos normally are considered the better of the two types of dwellings to put your money into. This chapter discusses the reasons for this.

What's the Difference?

What's the difference between a condo and a co-op? Physical differences can be slight, but ownership elements differ significantly. Most importantly, if you buy a condo, you receive a deed to prove ownership in real property. Buying a co-op gets you stock in a corporation, but no deed to real estate. You can sell your condo to anyone you wish, just as you could do a house, but the person buying your co-op may have to be approved by a board consisting of members of the corporation that owns the co-op building. Also, restrictions of owners' rights often are much more severe for co-op owners.

Condos are somewhat different from co-ops when it comes to what an owner can and cannot do with the property. If you buy a condo, you can make changes to the interior space. For example, if you don't like the kitchen cabinets and counters, you can replace them. Don't count on being able to do this in a co-op. I must stress that each planned development, whether a condo or co-op, can have individual rules, and you must be well aware of them before purchasing a unit to avoid problems down the road.

Condos and Co-ops vs. Other Forms of Ownership

Without going into a full-blown comparison of condos and co-ops, which could encompass a whole book in itself, let's talk about how the basic differences between these types of real estate and other forms of ownership affect you as an investment owner.

Condos and Co-ops as Rental Properties

In most cases, both condos and co-ops can be used as rental properties; however, restrictions placed on specific properties may limit or prohibit such use. This is why it's important that you check all of the documentation associated with any condo or co-op before you buy it. Again, developers and corporation owners set their own rules for their condos and co-ops. Don't assume anything. Prohibitions concerning nonowner-occupied units would be a disaster for an investor.

Rules in Abundance

Rules and bylaws are abundant when dealing with condos and co-ops. Although you can encounter covenants and restrictions attached to typical single-family homes, you can count on a long list of rules for condos and co-ops. For example, you might not be allowed to alter the address numbers on your exterior door or change a light fixture by your exterior door. Your choice in paint colors for the exterior of your unit might be limited. And having pets in your own space might be prohibited. The power of the rules is strong, and the number of rules can fill pages of paper. Once you are ready to buy a condo or co-op, look closely for all of the restrictions that may affect your plans.

Association Fees

Association fees (charged for maintenance of a condo or co-op development) and special assessments (levied when some improvement or repair is needed or desired) have the potential to ruin your investing budget when you own a condo or a co-op. You have no real control over the amounts of association fees and special assessments, which might have a disturbing effect on a building's cash flow. You may have a vote in how things will be done, but your vote will not, by itself, allow you to control your own destiny with a condo or a co-op. All you can do is hope for the best. You can look at historical data to build a reasonable assumption of what to expect in fee increases; unfortunately, a development that has been stable for the last ten years could go fee crazy after you buy into it. You simply have no guarantee, unless it's in your purchase agreement, to prevent fees from increasing regularly. This one factor alone is enough to scare some investors away from condos and co-ops.

Association fees usually are fair. They cover a variety of needs and relieve property owners of maintenance headaches. This is an advantage to investors when the fees are realistic and stable. However, because most developments don't have an annual cap on association fees, owners are at risk. And it's entirely possible that the fees could be raised on a more frequent basis than annually. For these reasons, be very careful of the fee structure if you buy a condo or a co-op. When you review the documents on a development, determine what the association fee covers. For example, do snow removal and lawn care for the development come out of the fee? Dig deeply to see exactly what your money pays for.

Special assessments usually are levied only for big-ticket items. If a building needs a repair that is costly and outside the scope of association fees, the price of the repair is placed on the shoulders of the owners of condos and co-ops within the development. Sometimes improvements are not necessary, but desired. For example, if the governing group decides to install a swimming pool, you could be required to pay for a portion of it, even if you don't support the decision or plan to use the amenity. In some cases, the debt is divided equally, but it also may be divided on a percentage basis, based on the degree of ownership. Have your lawyer pay close attention to all documents, but get a particularly strong opinion on association fees and special assessment regulations. For example, what rules pertain to special assessments? How likely are you to be hit with a big bill for resurfacing the parking lot? Will you be assessed for a roof repair or the installation of new playground equipment? Buying condos and co-ops where a number of amenities exist, such as tennis courts and swimming pools, can make a unit easier to rent, but it also puts you at higher risk for special assessment fees. The amenities will need maintenance and repair, and the property owners and shareholders will foot the bill.

Higher Risk

Although both can be riskier than other property types, co-ops usually are chancier than condos, mainly because co-op investors don't own real estate. As a co-op owner, you own stock in a corporation that owns the building in which your co-op is located. You submit your monthly payments, but the corporation still might fall into financial difficulty and file for protection under the bankruptcy laws. If this happens, you could lose all of your investment and your use of the co-op. This is not the case with a condo, where the owner maintains the mortgage on the individual unit.

The rules for selling stock in a co-op also can be much more rigid than general real estate law that governs the sale of condos and other property types. This is another reason a co-op can be riskier than a condo. Ask your lawyer to check all aspects of buying, renting, and selling either type of unit. Don't take anything for granted in real estate—especially when you are dealing with co-ops.

Co-ops, which exist primarily in large cities, have a mixed reputation as an investment vehicle. Like any purchase, co-ops require research and knowledge. If you plan to buy into co-ops, think long and hard before you purchase more than one or two of them in the same building. It's generally wiser to spread your ownership out among different developments.

When shopping for a co-op, look to buildings that have been in existence as co-ops for a few years. This allows you to research the history of the units. You can make bigger, faster money when you buy into new co-ops, but the risk is greater because you have no historical data on which to base your decision. Also look into the financial strength of the corporation that issues stock in the co-ops. You can ask the seller for this information. However, have a financial expert review the materials because the paperwork likely will be complicated.

Seasonal Units

More than other types of real estate, seasonal units in either condos or co-ops can produce lucrative incomes. Condos and co-ops in prime rental locations, such as ski areas and beach communities, don't come cheap, but they can be excellent investments. A unit that might rent for $750 a month in town as a year-round dwelling easily could fetch that same amount for a single week if it were located, say, across the street from the ocean. The downside to seasonal and vacation rentals is the labor intensive role of the landlord or manager, who must coordinate numerous short-term tenants.

A seasonal rental is just that—seasonal. This might mean that an owner's income stream ceases after a few months of use. However, many seasonal units can be rented for lower rates and longer terms during the off-season. It all comes down to money. If you can charge as much for a week with a seasonal as you would get for a month with a year-round unit, you don't need a long season to make the same amount of annual income, assuming you maintain a low vacancy rate during prime time. If you opt for a seasonal unit, though, be prepared to work at bringing in a lot of tenants for short stays. Some seasonal units are rented not by the week, but by the season. This lowers the rental amount, as a rule, but it cuts down on advertising costs, labor, and vacancies.

Here in Maine, cottages out on the islands and along the coast rent for high amounts during the summer, but they come quite cheap during the winter. Owners of the cottages can make enough in a couple of summer months to make their purchases viable, so the income for the rest of the year is all gravy. The same can be done with condos along beaches and in ski areas.

Buying condos or co-ops in recreational areas for seasonal rentals can make a lot of sense—and a lot of money. However, the risks of seasonal rentals can be greater in some years than in others. For example, if you own a condo on a ski slope during a year when very little snow falls, your profits might melt away like the snow you wish you had. Beachfront condos do much better in summers when frequent rain, fog, and similar bad weather are not problems. And let's not even mention hurricanes! Obviously, the weather can have a devastating effect on the income of recreational rentals. Because investors cannot predict the weather from one year to the next with certainty, seasonal rentals suffer from a risk that does not affect traditional rental property.

Condos and Co-ops: Not a Good Place to Start

Condos and co-ops probably are not a good place to start your career as a real estate investor. Of course, the two types of properties are used for investments all the time, and they can produce extremely well. If you buy into a development early, even in the preconstruction phase, the value of your unit can climb quickly. In fact, some investors specialize in reading the market and buying units before they are built. This often is called *buying units in the dirt*. The risk is high, but the rewards can be substantial. However, for an inexperienced investor the risk may be too high. It's easy to buy into an existing development and lose money, and it's even easier to buy into the plans for a development and lose money. Even if you are fortunate enough to buy into a sound development, the added burdens, rules, and regulations, not to mention the fees associated with condos and co-ops, can hinder your freedom as an investor.

Stories run rampant in investor circles about getting rich quick with condos and co-ops. And in the right market and with the right insights, you can get rich quick. I've seen investors buy units from blueprints and make close to $20,000 profit in less than 90 days. Some investors buy heavily into a single development in hopes of it being the mother lode of real estate. The strategy can pay off. If you own ten units and make $20,000 on each of them in six months, that equates to a profit of $200,000 in just half a year—and with passive income. Not bad! But if you misread the development and the units don't sell or rent well, you could be stuck in financial quicksand with nowhere to run and no money to drag you out.

The underlying risk of condos and co-ops make them both potentially lucrative and equally dangerous. As an investment consultant, I normally advise first-time investors to look at small apartment buildings as foundations for their rental portfolios. In certain cases, a condo or a co-op can be an excellent first investment, but the odds are higher that inexperienced investors will regret their purchases. As with a single-family home, it can be difficult to buy a condo or co-op that will produce enough rental income to carry its cost of ownership. If the market does not appreciate quickly and if the development is not popular, a condo or a co-op can drag you down.

If you move past houses, condos, and co-ops to start your investing career, the next logical building to consider is a duplex, the subject of our next chapter.

Investing in Duplexes

Duplexes (two-unit buildings) may well be one of the most sought after types of property for first-time investors—especially when the investors also are first-time homebuyers. A lot of people see the value of buying a duplex to live in one unit while renting out the other to reduce the overall cost of home ownership. When viewed in this light, duplexes make good sense. It's entirely possible to buy a duplex and within a few years to have the rental income paying most, and sometimes all, of the mortgage cost. It's hard to beat owning your own home and having someone else pay it off for you.

When you look at duplexes as straight investments that will not be owner occupied, they are not as desirable. This is not to say that they are not worthy investments, but the income a duplex produces does not always carry the cost of ownership. If you are working on a long-term goal and can afford to float a duplex in the early years, the building can be a great keeper. You can find duplexes that produce positive cash flow immediately; however, these opportunities are not common. If you can buy a single-family home and convert it into a duplex, the profit picture may become much brighter.

A lot of first-time investors like the idea of buying a duplex because of the price. Most duplexes cost more than comparable single-family homes, but less than buildings that contain more dwelling units. Because many first-time buyers are not fully aware of how real estate investing works, the lower price makes a convincing statement. In reality, a four-unit apartment building, even with the higher price tag, probably is a better value.

Duplexes often are considered an excellent way for investors to get their feet wet as landlords. Because no more than two units are rented out, the owner stands a good chance of being able to manage the property personally. If the landlord lives in one unit and rents out the other, management is even easier. Of course, living next door to your tenant can be uncomfortable. (We'll talk more about this a little later.)

You have many good reasons for buying a duplex—and some valid reasons not to purchase a two-unit building. Every real estate deal depends on several factors to become viable. Your personal goals may differ from mine or some other investor's. For this reason, you shouldn't rule out any type of real estate purchase until you and your attorney have examined the deal closely. With this in mind, let's explore duplexes as investments.

Advantages to Owning Duplexes

The advantages to buying a duplex include a low down payment if you will reside in the building, some rental income, and a place to live and call your own. These three factors influence many people to buy duplexes rather than single-family homes. Veterans usually can buy duplexes with no down payment. Nonveterans who plan to live in their duplexes generally need a down payment of no more than 5 percent of the purchase price.

Rental income from just one unit in a duplex can greatly reduce the cost of living for the property owner. In some cases, the single rental unit pays all of a duplex's ownership costs. Living in one duplex unit and renting out the other almost always is more cost effective than buying a single-family home.

If you will not live in your duplex, the investment may not be as appealing as it would be if the building were going to be your home. Buying a duplex as a nonoccupying investor typically requires a down payment of at least 20 percent of the purchase price. If you can swing this type of cash, the down payment will help make the building's numbers work. However, you might use the same amount of cash to obtain some creative financing on a larger building with more income potential. As a rookie investor, you must weigh all of your options before you jump into a buying decision.

No Free Rides

As stated above, duplexes are better investments for owners who will live in one half of the property. Nonowner-occupied rental property can make it hard to justify a duplex's numbers. Of course, it all depends on the purchase price, financing, and rental rates that investors can command. Most professional real estate investors pass over duplexes for larger buildings. The time and effort spent on them is not worth the reward for investors who can handle larger, more expensive properties. This opens a window of opportunity for beginning investors. If you have enough time to look for a good deal, you probably will find a duplex that produces a positive cash flow.

It is often said that life offers no free rides. Although duplexes sometimes seem to be the ultimate free ride when it comes to housing, usually they are not. Too many investors believe that when they live in one unit, the tenant in the other unit pays all of the costs of ownership via the rent the owner collects. True, some investors find duplexes that support themselves when both units are rented, but the odds of buying a duplex that pays for itself with just one tenant are not favorable. Even if you build a duplex yourself, from the ground up, you probably would have difficulty getting a single unit to pay for both dwellings. Keep in mind, though, that even one tenant pays a large percentage of your ownership costs. Financially speaking, this is much better than living in a single-family home, where you must pay the entire mortgage amount.

As stated earlier, trying to find a duplex that carries its own costs with two tenants is not easy, but it can be done. In fact, you have several ways to improve the odds of creating such a deal. One way is to build the duplex yourself. Another ideal way might be to find a single-family home that is zoned for two families. If the house is suitable for conversion to a duplex, you just might hit paydirt. Buying a rundown duplex and fixing it up, especially if you can do the work yourself, is another good way to create a positive cash flow in a hurry. Because duplexes are popular, ready-to-live-in properties usually command high enough prices to make positive cash flows unlikely.

Living Next Door to Your Tenants

One disadvantage of owning and living in a duplex could be your proximity to your tenant. Being a landlord can be tough enough under any conditions. A landlord who lives next door to his tenant may have it much worse. Even if your tenant is a pleasant person, easy to get along with, living next to him might mean having your privacy invaded frequently. You're so handy. If a bulb burns out in the porch light, you likely will hear a knock at your door. Your tenant might pop in during your dinner to tell you that the toilet in the rental unit is stopped up. And if you are unfortunate enough to have to evict your tenant, living beside him can be extremely stressful.

As bad as living next to a tenant can be, the principle can also work in your favor. Sometimes living next door to your tenant actually makes management chores easier. Landlords who manage their own properties usually visit the properties often for one reason or another.

When you run a duplex and live in half of it, you require no travel time to get to your property. If you have to change a light bulb or show the rental unit to a prospective tenant, you don't have to leave home to do it. Collecting rent is a snap. And it's much easier to keep a watchful eye on how a tenant treats your property when you live under the same roof. Tenants, too, are more likely to be on their best behavior.

Living in a duplex that you share with a tenant can put some stress on the tenant-landlord relationship. If you and your tenant don't get along socially it can be quite uncomfortable to share common grounds. For this reason, many duplex investors try to find tenants who can be friends. However, if you and your tenant become buddies, it can make enforcing your landlord rules unpleasant for you. It's hard to evict or collect past-due rent from a friend. Other landlords choose tenants based on the tenants' potential to become part-time property managers when the duplex owners move onto other buildings and allow their duplexes to become straight rental properties. Investors who groom tenants to become on-site managers often enjoy low-maintenance careers as investors.

As an investor, I have shared a roof with some of my tenants. From a landlord's perspective, the arrangements worked well for me. However, being a person who enjoys solitude, I soon gave up my role as live-in landlord and began building houses, first to live in, then to rent out. I would build a new house, live in it about a year, build another new house, then use the first house as rental property. This way, I made a little money building the houses, kept my investment low enough to make the rental income viable, and got a new house each year. This worked well for me, but some people wouldn't want to move as often as I did.

A friend of mine who was a carpenter, a land developer, and a real estate investor spent his off-season building duplexes that he was willing to sell or rent. I worked with him as a consultant. My friend did very well for himself with the duplexes. Most of what he built sold quickly because he chose prime locations for construction, designed modern and spacious living areas, and contributed to closing costs and points. The duplexes my friend kept in his portfolio rented quickly and profitably. By designing the duplex units to resemble single-family homes, the developer attracted high-quality tenants willing to pay top rental rates. For an extra monthly fee, tenants were allowed to keep pets in the units. This increased income and reduced tenant turnover. Because my friend had the ability to build his own duplexes, without any need for a general contractor, he was able to generate positive cash flow from his projects, even without living on site.

Moving up the Real Estate Ladder

Moving up the ladder of real estate investing doesn't mean you must give up good duplexes. When you are ready to move on to larger buildings, you can retain ownership of your two-unit buildings. In fact, duplexes can make good stepping stones to larger buildings. If a duplex has keeper potential, keep it. Sell buildings that don't offer keeper potential to generate cash to buy larger buildings. When you own a duplex, you get a little taste of what it's like to be a landlord. Even such a small piece of the pie can tell you if you want more. It's entirely possible that after owning a duplex, you will never want to deal with rental tenants again. However, you might enjoy the work and wish to buy additional units. For this reason, duplexes are perfect first investments: they supply you with a place to live and provide a feel for what it's like to be a landlord.

Many investors buy duplexes with the intent of living in them so that a lower down payment is required. This doesn't mean that the investors must live in the duplexes for long. Loan regulations vary, but in most cases, even residing in a duplex for a few weeks meets loan criteria. Then the investor can rent out both units of the duplex while she buys another duplex to live in. Generally, this strategy is perfectly legal and can be a great way to buy into duplexes with down payments of about 5 percent of the purchase prices. Before you try this, though, check with your attorney to learn your local laws and your lender's regulations.

Investors often buy small rental properties, then move into them for a few months. This gives the investors time to improve the properties while they live on site. Sometimes an investor uses this time to adjust a building's tenant situation. Once the property is up and running, the investor buys another building and moves on, renting out the unit the investor had lived in. As long as a building generates a positive cash flow, it doesn't compromise an investor's ability to leave and buy another property. This approach is very effective for investors working with very little cash and a lot of creativity.

If you keep your duplexes as you move on to larger buildings, the duplexes have time to appreciate in value, and rental rates tend to escalate to help generate a more positive cash flow. Normally, selling a building a year or two after you buy it yields very little profit, so hold onto your duplexes if it is possible. However, if you are looking to sell a duplex, you shouldn't have any shortage of potential buyers. Having been in the real estate business for as long as I have, I can tell you that a voracious appetite exists among small-scale investors and homebuyers for duplexes.

Duplexes Sell Like Hotcakes

One advantage to duplexes is that they sell well in most markets. If you are just wading into the investing waters, consider duplexes to be relatively safe, shallow water. You can lose money on a duplex, but most of them sell quickly if they are priced right. The lure of a place to live with a tenant to pay much of the housing expense is a primary reason duplexes move briskly. This is good if you are a seller, but not so good if you are a buyer. Most duplexes in good shape command steep sales prices. This is why it's good to be willing to take on rehab projects and to dig for properties that hold the potential for conversion to duplexes.

If they have to rent, tenants often prefer to live in duplexes rather than apartments. While duplexes normally don't offer the same amenities that an apartment complex might, the quiet, peaceful elements of a duplex make the rental space desirable. In fact, it's not unusual for duplex units to command higher rents than the same square footage would bring in a larger building. This helps offset the higher per-unit cost of buying a duplex. Many investors also feel that duplexes pull higher quality tenants who stay longer than apartment dwellers do.

Because duplexes contain only two rental units, they tend to be easier to manage than larger buildings. As long as the tenants in each half of the duplex get along well enough with each other, management problems can be minimal. Duplexes consisting of side-by-side rental units often are favored over those whose rental units are stacked. This is due largely to the reduced noise between the tenants. It's far more intrusive to hear people walking overhead than it is to have them off to one side.

Tenant relations is a big part of being a successful landlord. When you run small buildings, it is easier to match tenants who will be compatible. Trying to find tenants to fill a 12-unit building who will all get along is much harder than finding tenants who can tolerate each other in a duplex. All of these reasons combine to make duplexes desirable to investors who prefer to work on a personal basis with their tenants and on a smaller scale.

Buildings deemed attractive to investors command high selling prices. This is the case with duplexes. Very few major-league investors rely on duplexes to float their financial boats, but an awful lot of beginning real estate investors are in the market to buy duplexes. If you are new to real estate and are not sure how long you want to stay in the business, a duplex should be a safe starting point. Cash flow likely will be better with a larger building, but a duplex is a relatively inexpensive way to test the waters as a first-time landlord.

CHAPTER 11

Three-Unit and Four-Unit Buildings: Ideal First Investments

Many experienced investors think three-unit and four-unit buildings are ideal first-time investments. Buying a four-unit building (quad) can be as easy as buying a single-family home, and the quad offers superior profit potential. Three-unit buildings (triplexes) are the middle ground between duplexes and quads. Think of the number of rental units as increments of profit. Normally, the more rental units you own, the more money you make. Four-unit buildings are a bit more popular than triplexes because they can be financed with the same types of loans, may not cost much more, and provide an additional rental unit to generate profit.

Duplexes work for owners who occupy them, but hands-off investors often have trouble turning a profit. Making money gets easier with triplexes, but investors still may encounter plenty of risk and tight numbers. Some triplexes produce more net income than some quads; however, logically speaking, more units equal more income. Moving up to a four-unit building increases the odds of success. Either building—triplex or quad—can prove profitable. Cost compared to return should be similar. Triplexes bring in less money, but they usually don't cost as much as quads. You must evaluate every project on a case-by-case basis. All aspects of real estate investment are subject to specific, individual conditions.

Pros and Cons of Triplexes and Quads

We talked in the last chapter about duplexes and their pros and cons. Much of the information pertaining to duplexes also applies to triplexes. Circumstances begin to change more when you get into four-unit buildings; however, until you exceed four rental units you can finance a quad like you can a house. This means a required down payment as low as 5 percent of the purchase price if you plan to oc- cupy the property. Most lenders will allow you to claim some por- tion of the rental income from the apartment building to offset your loan requirements in terms of qualifying ratios. Therefore, it actually can be easier to buy a four-unit building than a duplex. The quad should cost more than the duplex, but the added rental income can more than compensate for the increased cost. This is something many new investors are not aware of.

As a broker, I've worked with untold numbers of first-time in- vestors. By far, a majority of them think they are limited to small buildings, like duplexes, due to overall purchase price. They can't imagine that a lender will allow them to buy larger buildings that cost maybe twice as much. Generally, their fears are unfounded. Be- cause a lender uses a building's rental income, based on historical data, the qualification process for a loan can be easier with a big building than a smaller property. In fact, you might be able to buy a 6-unit or a 12-unit apartment building with less out-of-pocket cash than it would take to buy a duplex that you didn't plan to live in. Cer- tainly, bigger buildings cost more and require larger down payments (for example, 5 percent of a quad's sales price amounts to more than the same percentage of a duplex's price); however, depending on how a deal is structured and how financing is arranged, you could buy into larger buildings with less money. Larger buildings often fall under commercial loan status, which means the seller may hold a second mortgage for part of the down payment.

Deciding on what type of real estate to invest in is not easy. No one can tell you which projects offer the most profit or potential. Results vary depending on numerous factors. Investors must seek their own levels. Usually, buying small apartment buildings is an excellent way to create wealth; however, when inexperienced investors move into a market coveted by high-rolling investors—such as the market for quads and larger buildings—the risk can become greater. Sharks working the waters of real estate investments sometimes go into feeding frenzies.

No real estate investor is guaranteed safety. You could be taken advantage of when buying a single-family home. A savvy investor might sell you a duplex with conditions that don't favor your position. You have no way to know which baits contain the hooks when you happen upon them. However, the right research and patience can help keep you safe when purchasing smaller properties. But as you move up to larger buildings, you are more likely to be dealing with professionals who make their livings buying and selling real estate. For this reason, treat every deal like a dangerous one (even deals to purchase smaller properties, for that matter). Learn to work with historical data, research materials, and your attorney to weed out the bad projects. The quicker you have your radar, the more likely you are to be successful.

To protect yourself, learn all you can about a property. Evaluate such things as:

- Incomplete expense reports
- Physical defects in the property
- Building code violations
- Neighborhood positioning
- Desirability of location

- Exaggerated income reports
- Expiring leases
- Liens on the property
- Appraised value
- Market comparables
- Any historical data you can compile

Buy It Like a House

The nice thing about a triplex or a quad is that you can buy it like a house. If you plan to live in the building, you can find lenders that will offer loans requiring low down payments. Interest rates on buildings housing two to four units also can be as low as they would be for single-family homes. The borrowing process for buildings with four or fewer units is quite easy for people who will occupy the properties.

Aside from being easy, buying a triplex or a quad can be cost effective and profitable. Don't expect to have extreme flexibility in creative financing with these buildings, though—especially if you don't plan to occupy the property. Many lenders sell their loans for small apartment buildings (fewer than five units) on the secondary mortgage market; therefore, the loan requirements must meet the market's strict rules. Some lenders, however, service their own loans and do not sell them, so they can be quite creative in their financing. For example, you might be able to arrange for the seller to hold a substantial second mortgage that reduces your down payment requirements. You and your lender agree on the terms of an in-house, portfolio loan. As long as you make the lender comfortable with the terms, anything is possible.

If you have the status to obtain a VA loan, you might be able to buy up to a four-unit building with nearly no down payment. An adjustable-rate mortgage (ARM) also can be a good choice. And it's fairly easy to obtain an FHA loan, where the down payment can be less than 5 percent of the purchase price. These conditions are based on the fact that the purchaser will reside in the property being bought. If you do not plan to occupy the building you are buying, a down payment of 20 percent of the purchase price likely will be required. If the lender will sell the loan to the secondary mortgage market, a seller willing to hold paper on the deal can do so, but the full amount of the down payment must come from you, not from the seller in the form of a second mortgage.

Best Buys

Best buys in real estate come in all shapes and sizes. A shopping mall, raw land, or an apartment building can be a best buy for your portfolio. But many investors concentrate their efforts on residential properties that can be financed like single-family homes— duplexes, triplexes, and quads. Of these, four-unit buildings often are the target because they offer the most income potential.

Buying buildings that can be financed like houses makes a lot of sense for investors who will live in the buildings. Buying an apartment building with a down payment of 5 percent or less is a deal that's hard to resist. However, entering into a deal with very little money can make it difficult to generate a positive cash flow. If you will use the building as a home *and* as a cash-producing investment, the pendulum swings in your direction. A profit-only investor would need positive cash flow or growing equity to justify a purchase. This is not the case if your investment is also your home. Most people buy single-family homes to live in, the only major rewards being growing equity and some tax advantages. If you buy a multifamily building to live in, you get these same advantages, plus rental income and probably some additional tax benefits.

People who buy single-family homes to live in make investments in these properties. Most homeowners get tax advantages when they finance their houses. They also tend to see the homes' value increase over time. These two factors alone make the purchase of a home sensible. However, if you can get these benefits and have tenants who will pay for most, if not all, of your housing expenses, the investment becomes much more lucrative.

Seeking Positive Cash Flow

Most investors seek positive cash flow; however, the elusive trail to profit can be hard to define and follow. Will you find prosperity in real estate? If you are willing to work at it, you should be able to make money as an investor. How much you will make and where you will make it constitute your individual investment plan. Some investors do it with quick-flips; others do it with keepers. Buildings consisting of three or four units can fall into either category.

A building's size, condition, and location directly affect how much money the building has the potential to produce. Typically, bigger buildings have higher sales prices than smaller buildings. However, smaller buildings often cost more on a per-unit basis than larger buildings. In most cases, the value of triplexes and quads is computed with methods similar to those used to calculate the value of single-family homes. A direct income approach to appraisal normally is not used for smaller apartment buildings.

For Example . . .

For the sake of our example, let's say that the duplex is worth $65,000 per unit, or $130,000 in total. The triplex is worth $57,000 per unit, or $171,000. The four-unit building has a per-unit value of $53,000, or $212,000. Without going into detail on all of the ownership costs, let's see how the payoff works. We will not compute operating expenses, taxes, and so forth;

we simply will work with monthly mortgage amounts and rents. Assume a 20 percent down payment on each building and all units occupied by tenants at a rental rate of $600 a month. The buildings are financed for 30 years at an interest rate of 8.25 percent.

The duplex's monthly payment is $781.32. With an income of $1,200 a month, this generates a nice profit. Of course, in real life, expenses would reduce the profit. A monthly cost of $1,027.73 is due on the triplex. The $1,800 of income plays nicely. With a payment of $1,274.15 due on the quad, there is income of $2,400. So what does all of this mean?

In the case of the duplex, the mortgage cost equals about 65 percent of the gross income. The triplex cost equals about 57 percent of the gross income. Using the same formula, the four-unit building shows a cost of 53 percent of the gross. You would not work with these figures to make a buying decision because they are incomplete, but they are fair and illustrate at a glance how the larger buildings produce stronger incomes. However, you also must consider the amount of money invested in each building as a down payment. The down payment on the duplex would total $26,000. In the case of the triplex, the out-of-pocket money amounts to $34,200. The down payment on the four-unit building equals $42,400. ∎

As you can see, the cash invested escalates with the price of each building. This investment of a higher down payment does pay off in terms of stronger cash flow. If you have enough money to make large down payments, you create safer investment environments. Buying into a building with a small down payment can set the stage for financial difficulties. It's a good plan to spread out available cash and to work with multiple investments when things work the way you want them to, but it's a fast track to failure when things go wrong.

Less Risk with Small Rental Properties

Generally, it is considered safer to invest in three-unit and four-unit buildings when you are starting out and gaining experience as an investor. In fact, buying a triplex or a quad is about the safest way I know of to get into rental property as a landlord. The risk of buying a triplex or quad is reduced even more when it doubles as your home. At the very least, you will have a place to live and should have rental income to help make your payments. Let's assume that you buy the four-unit building we talked about earlier—the one with the monthly payment of $1,274. If you rent out three of the units for $600 each, you have a gross income of $1,800. Even after paying basic ownership expenses, you have a chance of breaking even on the deal, and you could be living rent and mortgage free. Of course, if you opted for a smaller down payment, the numbers would change.

If you put only 5 percent down on the building, the monthly payment would be about $1,513. Your income, however, still would be $1,800. By the time you paid real estate taxes, insurance, utilities, and such, you would have a negative cash flow. Even so, the amount of money you would have to shell out would be a cost-effective "house payment."

Small Rental Properties Are Serious Investments

Don't fall into the trap of thinking that residential-grade rental properties—such as quads and triplexes—are not serious investments. The money you spend and the money you make on a small building is just as real as the money you spend and earn on bigger deals. A profit is a profit, regardless of its size. The goal of investing is simple: making money. Granted, it is more fun to earn $50,000 than it is to make $500, but profit is proportionate to risk and effort.

Any time a person puts hard-earned money on the line in hopes of making more money, the deal is serious. Losing $15,000 on a duplex hurts just as much as losing it on a major condo development. To be successful, you must treat every deal with respect and a degree of caution. Buying a $100,000 building that turns out to be a loser will sink your ship a lot faster than spending $500,000 on a winner. Never underestimate the power of small buildings. Net profit is much more important than gross income.

Apartment buildings with four or fewer units make excellent stepping stones and can stand alone as investments. You can use the buildings to establish yourself as an investor in various ways. Living in one building for awhile, then moving into a new building and renting out the first building works for some investors. Other investors buy several small buildings instead of one big building. By spreading out their ownership, they spread out their risk.

An investor who works wisely with small apartment buildings can create a tremendous power base for wealth. You don't have to buy multi-million-dollar projects to make millions of dollars. In fact, it is sometimes easier to make more money with smaller projects than it is to turn the same profits with bigger deals. People often think that their profits must be in direct proportion to the size of their investments. This is not always the case. In fact, appreciation rates often are higher, on a percentage basis, for smaller buildings than for larger buildings. A big apartment building might appreciate at a rate of 3 percent a year, while a four-unit building may climb in value at 7 percent per year. Of course, even a smaller percentage rate on a much more expensive building can amount to more money. There is still money to be made with smaller buildings, though. Don't shrug off their profit potential. Learn how to create it and go for it.

Small buildings also fit the profile for different types of investments. You can buy them as rehab projects, conversion projects, or midterm or long-term keepers. You can even buy them with residential financing programs and live in them. This versatility is a strong reason to justify the purchase of smaller buildings.

In terms of finding a good starting place as an investor, you probably can't do better than a small apartment building. This is especially true if you plan to live in it. If you already live in a single-family home and seek cash-producing investments, smaller buildings are still viable. Given the right sales price, income and expenses, you can make money with any type of property. Don't rule out small buildings when you structure your rental plans. For many, a four-unit apartment building is an ideal first investment.

CHAPTER *12*

Five-Unit and
Ten-Unit Buildings

Investors who move up to commercial-grade buildings—those housing five or more apartments—can make much more money than investors who stick with residential-grade properties. Although there is no guarantee that bigger buildings will produce more profits, logic points to the fact that larger properties offer more earning potential because more units should produce more income. However, bigger buildings also can mean bigger headaches. Before you move into a larger building, you must make sure you are ready for the added risk and responsibility.

I've worked with a large number of first-time investors. Many of them have bought residential-grade properties, but a lot have purchased larger units. It may be coincidence, but investors who have bought six-unit buildings have proved to be the most successful. Frankly, I believe that six-unit buildings are an ideal size for investors with sufficient time and knowledge who want manageable properties that offer enough rental units to produce substantial positive cash flow. Six-unit buildings cost more than smaller buildings and require more attention due to the number of units; however, they usually provide enough income basis to carry a vacancy without generating a negative cash flow. Investors who have experience as landlords definitely have an advantage when it comes to being successful with rental properties, but it is possible for novice investors to learn as they go.

The Big Leagues: Pros and Cons

If you decide to get into the big leagues of larger buildings, you will compete with many experienced investors. The good news is that this tells you that you are on the right track to finding the money in real estate. The bad news is that you may not be prepared to face the level of competition. Don't be frightened. Almost any adult can learn to compete for larger buildings. You don't have to be a seasoned investor to make money with commercial-grade properties.

Getting into bigger buildings can require you to have more money than you would need to buy, say, a duplex. Due to the larger price tags, the down payment requirements are higher. However, with the right approach and some seller financing, you *might* be able to get into a larger building with even less cash than you would need to buy a smaller residential-grade property. You've already read about how I've helped some investors walk away from their closings with more money than they had when they sat down at the table. Keep in mind, though, that closing on a larger building with little to no money isn't always easy.

One advantage to buying larger buildings is the fact that the financing can be much more creative than the financing for residential loans that will be sold on the secondary mortgage market. Commercial lenders sometimes will stretch normal lending rules to make a deal. When you buy a building that meets commercial status (including a residential apartment building with five or more units), the property can stand on its own. By this, I mean that your income from your job may not be as important as the building's history as an income producer. Let's consider an example.

For Example . . .

Let's assume that you are buying a building that houses eight rental units. The property is in good shape, has stable tenants, and has shown strong income for the last several years. The building's vacancy rate is very low, and maintenance and repair expenses also have been below average—all in all, a strong property. Now assume that you have arranged partial seller financing. You seek a bank loan of only 70 percent of the property's appraised value. ∎

Based on our assumptions, a lender should jump at the chance to finance the building—but will the bank loan money to you? If you have no experience as a landlord, the lender may be leery. You have a way to make the bank rest more comfortably, however. Suppose you retain a proven property management firm to handle the building for you. This overcomes your lack of experience, both in the real world and on paper. Paying a management company will eat into your profits, but it may nudge the bank to offer you the loan.

If the building produces enough income to cover the cost of a management firm, the bank shouldn't hold your lack of experience against you. Typical management rates run about 10 percent of a building's gross rental income, plus charges for specialized services, such as renting vacant apartments, managing subcontractors performing maintenance and repairs, and so forth. Once you own the building and demonstrate your ability to oversee the property management firm, you can purchase more buildings. In time, you will have the experience needed to make bankers relax when you want to buy and manage a building yourself. The advantages of hiring a management firm are many, with the only major disadvantage being the cost.

Being the landlord of a single-family home can be more difficult than managing a 12-unit apartment building. Real estate management varies from property to property and from tenant to tenant. First-time investors often think they can handle a triplex, but not a six-unit building. True, the additional three units point to more potential problems, but the problems may never occur. Don't fall into the trap of believing that small buildings are easy to manage and larger buildings are difficult. This assumption has no real basis. Ease of management is related to the quality of your buildings and tenants. If you have the time, money, and drive to make your properties work for you, don't let building size hold you back.

Large Rental Properties Mean Serious Money

You can make a lot of money with large rental buildings because more rental units usually equate to more money. This is not always the case, but often it is. One large building can produce as much annual profit as a person might earn working full time every week of the year. If this doesn't seem fair, don't cast your opinion too quickly. Running a big building is not easy; a lot of work is involved. Even if a management firm handles most of the day-to-day chores for you, it still is up to you to oversee and direct the management company.

I've known many investors who make their livings from their rental buildings—but don't quit your day job just yet. It's much easier to buy buildings when you have steady employment outside of the rental business. Your goal may be to become a full-time landlord, but don't rush it. Serious money is at stake. After you gain experience as an investor and a landlord, the job gets easier.

Build a solid rental portfolio gradually, and begin to live off of your rental earnings. The money is good when you buy the right buildings and run them properly. The biggest mistake I've seen is investors' desire to get too big too quick. Growth is good, but ballooning overnight can be disastrous. The risk is greatest when you have very little equity in the properties you buy.

Creative Financing Options

The financing options for commercial-grade buildings are limited only by your imagination and your lender's willingness. Really, anything goes with big buildings, as long as all the parties agree to the terms. For example, a seller of a commercial-grade property can hold a second mortgage to reduce the amount of cash you need to buy the building. You also might find a lender willing to loan the full amount of your purchase price if the price is well below the real estate's appraised value. Some lenders—gamblers by nature—are more interested in making money from interest rates than placing conservative, secure loans. Finally, you can use equity in other buildings as collateral for commercial loans. The only limits are those you and your lender place on a deal.

Some lenders will not work with creative financing. Other lenders welcome the opportunity. Some lenders don't want to touch commercial deals. They work in the secondary mortgage market and won't take loans they can't sell. Simply put, they don't want to service the loans. Other lenders specialize in commercial loans. For these reasons—and plenty more—you must shop for the right lender. Don't limit yourself to your local bank; talk to a number of bank representatives. And don't concentrate all of your efforts on banks; explore mortgage bankers and mortgage brokers. Ask about loan policies from all legitimate lenders that make loans in the area where your proposed building is located. Leave no stone unturned. If you plan to buy a number of buildings in the coming years, you will benefit greatly from working with more than one lender. A lender that welcomes you with open arms when you buy a six-unit building may have no interest in working with you when you propose a four-unit building.

Bigger Buildings, Bigger Risk?

It might seem natural to assume that bigger buildings mean bigger risk; however, this is not always the case. When you invest in large rental properties you encounter different types of problems than you might experience with smaller buildings. Having ten rental units, for example, is a big responsibility, but if a tenant moves out, you still have nine tenants to cover your expenses. If one tenant moves out of a duplex, the duplex almost certainly would lose money until the tenant is replaced. The same could happen with a bigger building, but the odds of surviving a long-term vacancy are better.

Vacancies are only one risk associated with rental properties. Suppose you own one ten-unit building, compared with an investor who owns five duplexes in different areas. You run the risk that your large building will not be in a desirable location. This would affect your bottom line to a greater degree than the duplex owner's if one duplex was located poorly. However, if you do your homework before you buy a building, you will know whether the location is suitable. To determine a good location, track rental histories through local newspapers, explore the neighborhood at all times of the day and night, talk to brokers and appraisers, consult with other investors, and evaluate sales histories.

Commercial-grade properties boast larger, more expensive mechanical systems, but there might be more risk in owning many small buildings with numerous HVAC systems.

The list of risks could go on and on. The pendulum can swing both ways, but large buildings seem to be no riskier than small buildings—unless you are a new investor. I rarely recommend buildings with more than 10 or 12 units for investors who are just starting out. It is my opinion that anything larger than that is more than an average investor can handle without the assistance of a professional management firm. Even then, the investor may not possess the knowledge to oversee the management company.

Moving up to Large Rental Properties

If you are on the verge of moving up to a larger building, you should feel proud. A certain amount of personal satisfaction comes with buying such property. Driving up to a ten-unit apartment building and knowing that you own it can be quite rewarding. It's easy to build a case for buying bigger buildings. They offer more money, less risk, and greater prestige, to name a few reasons to take the plunge. It is not difficult to talk yourself into buying real estate; however, it can be hard to control yourself so that you buy only the right buildings. Don't let the overpowering influence and allure of real estate intoxicate you. It's crucial that you maintain a level head at all times when you are an investor.

If you buy a building with more than ten rental units, you set yourself up for a lot of responsibility. You probably should hire a professional management team to run a building of this size, unless you have the qualities needed to do the job yourself. You don't have to be a proven landlord to run large buildings, but some traits prove quite helpful.

Organizational skills are a must for landlords who run larger buildings. You must be capable of keeping all aspects of your rental business in good order. This can mean filing, bookkeeping, scheduling appointments, and much more. If you have a natural talent for organization, you have at least one of the qualities needed to run a large building.

How are your people skills? With a large building, you will come into contact with many tenants and prospective tenants. You will settle disputes, negotiate contracts, and collect rent. Will you function well in your role of manager? You must explore your feelings, your strengths, and your weaknesses to determine where you fit in as a landlord. It may be best for you to rely on a management company to handle your properties.

Buying bigger buildings calls for more time than is required with smaller buildings. Of all the elements needed to be a good landlord, time may be the one that most often derails investors in the early stages of their careers. A lot of people have no idea how much time is really needed to deal with management issues. For instance, can you meet plumbers and electricians during the day for repairs? How difficult will it be for you to show vacant apartments to tenants? Being organized helps reduce a landlord's time requirements, but plenty of demands on a landlord's time remain. The best plan is to buy a building that will support a management company's services. Then you can try managing the building on your own and bring in a management company if the task proves too much for you. The key is buying smart and managing well.

Fixer-Uppers Can Be Gold Mines

Fixer-uppers could be your ticket to riches beyond your imagination. You can make a lot of money just buying and selling real estate, but fixing up the properties between the buying and the selling can send profits off the charts. Fixer-upper properties can take any form. A single-family home can offer plenty of potential, as can a retail property or an apartment building. If an investor has the skills to do much of the fix-up work by himself, the profits can be staggering. In a matter of just a few months, the investor can earn tens of thousands of dollars.

Having been involved with construction and remodeling for much of my adult life, it is easy to see why I favor fixer-uppers. My personal abilities allow me to do much of the work needed to turn a rundown property into a real estate jewel. However, I have found over the years that even though I have the ability to do much of the work myself, I often hire others to do the job for me. This is good news for investors who are not hands-on remodelers. You don't have to be a carpenter, a plumber, or an electrician to make money with fixer-uppers.

The fixer-upper market is strong throughout the year. Seasonal changes don't directly affect a project's potential profitability. This is one reason people who work in the building trades flock to fixer-uppers. For example, carpenters who work in extreme climates often buy fixer-uppers to keep them busy in the winter, when they must confine their work to the indoors. Other contractors work on fixer-uppers in their off seasons. It's a lucrative way to stay busy in otherwise slow times.

Because fixer-uppers require work and can be difficult to finance, many investors pass them by. Some lenders won't loan money on rundown buildings, burned-out buildings, or buildings that are not structurally sound. They are interested only in more typical loan types. Don't let this discourage you. Commercial banks, as well as other lenders, welcome acquisition and improvement loans.

You may encounter considerable competition for fixer-uppers, but you can beat out many competitors by looking for properties when they are not. If you are out buying while contractors are trying to keep up with their seasonal workloads, you can find some good deals with less competition. Even if you must shop for properties in the prime selling season, the competition for fixer-uppers is still lighter than it is for other types of properties.

It takes a special type of person to work with houses that are not fit to live in or buildings that need substantial improvements. You don't have to be good at working with your hands necessarily, but you should possess certain qualities. For example, you need patience, strong organizational skills, and an ability to manage people. You also require enough money to tide you over while your fixer-upper generates no cash flow. If you can manage the work of others, you can become your own general contractor and pocket the money that a professional contractor would charge to oversee a job—typically about 20 percent of the total cost of labor and materials. Couple this with some attractive grants and low-interest loans that usually are available and you are on the road to riches.

Working with Your Own Hands

Having the ability to remodel a property yourself adds a lot of value to the work that goes into a fixer-upper. As discussed above, you can save up to 20 percent of an improvement's appraised value without ever picking up a paint brush or hammer if you act as your own general contractor. If you can do the work yourself, you also can pocket the money you would spend for labor. The cost of labor varies from trade to trade and from region to region, but usually it is a handsome sum. For example, with plumbers charging between $18 and $100 an hour, it's easy to see how doing the plumbing work in your own property yourself could save you a lot of money. The same could be said for electrical work and numerous other professional services.

Most people without construction experience who want to do some of their own work to save money pick painting. Applying paint properly can be an art form, but it is a job that most anyone can do. In addition to painting, cleaning, landscaping, and other elements of a major remodeling job all can be tackled by a person with modest skills.

I've often built new houses and remodeled fixer-uppers under a plan that allowed me to profit immediately. Basically, I financed the street value of the work. By obtaining financing based on full appraised value and acting as my own general contractor, I financed enough to pay myself about 20 percent of the cost of the work. Because my loan was based on the going rate for the work, I was able to pay myself out of the loan when I did the work myself. This gave me a cash flow, but it left little equity in the building. If you do your own work and don't pay yourself for your time, you build strong equity in the property you are remodeling. In time, you may have enough equity to leverage the equity as purchase money for another project.

If you are a handy person willing to work with fixer-uppers, you can make money in three ways:

1. Most investors make money by buying and selling real estate, including fixer-uppers.
2. General contractors make money by arranging and managing the work of others. You, too, can make money acting as your own contractor on a fixer-upper.
3. Tradespeople earn money by working with their hands. Again, you can cash in on this element by fixing up your own fixer-upper.

Anyone who has the ability to perform construction and remodeling work should give a serious look at fixer-uppers.

To Be or Not to Be a General Contractor

Not everyone fancies the idea of drilling holes, cutting lumber, sanding drywall compound, and running electrical wires. Some people don't like the idea of getting dirty. Some professionals must be especially sensitive to hurting their hands. Some people can make more money doing other things with their time; therefore, it is simply more cost effective to pay someone else to do work for them. Any of these reasons sets the stage for an investor either to hire a general contractor or to act as one in a fixer-upper's renovation or repair.

Working with subcontractors in various trades is not easy. In fact, it can be quite frustrating. Subcontractors don't always show up when they are supposed to, for example. And sometimes their work is not acceptable. Running complete remodeling crews can be a full-time job, depending on the volume of work, yet an investor can save money by doing so. As stated above, it's not uncommon for general contractors to tack an additional 20 percent onto all of the labor and material costs as compensation for services rendered. You can keep this money for yourself if you are willing to wear a general contractor's hat.

A general contractor should have a good understanding of the work being performed by others to be a good supervisor; however, the general contractor's credentials need not contain hands-on experience. Almost anyone can assume the role of general contractor and enjoy success, assuming she is committed to getting the job done right and on time. Books about remodeling, building, and related trades can be of great help to an inexperienced general contractor.

If you decide to act as your own general contractor, you should have strong organizational abilities, leadership qualities, and people skills, as well as a willingness to play hard ball when needed. Don't rule out being a general contractor solely because you have little to no experience in the trades. If you can arrange things and manage workers effectively, you can be a general contractor.

In theory, general contractors need not know how to perform any aspect of building or remodeling themselves. It should be possible to retain qualified subcontractors to execute whatever work is needed. In real life, a general contractor should have at least a basic understanding of the work being done. Sometimes this knowledge is necessary for a general contractor to keep the subcontractors honest in their work performance. For example, a plumber says it will take two days to set fixtures in one bathroom; however, the general contractor knows that an experienced plumber can trim out a tub-shower combination installed during a rough-in phase in less than 30 minutes. A master plumber can set a typical toilet in about 15 minutes. The installation of a lavatory bowl and faucet should take less than an hour. Based on this, a professional plumber should be able to set fixtures in a typical bathroom in no more than a couple of hours. Yet if a general contractor didn't know better, the two-day time estimate might seem reasonable. If an inexperienced general contractor fell into the grasp of unscrupulous subcontractors, the cost of a job could far exceed what it should be.

If you have no idea of what to expect from subcontractors, don't worry; you have ways to protect yourself. You can buy cost guides at most book stores that estimate the time needed for various types of work. You also could hire a construction or remodeling consultant to talk with when you have concerns. But getting bids from at least three contractors is the best way to protect yourself. Multiple bids allow you to nail down your expected costs and weed out the contractors that are both much too cheap and much too expensive.

If you have the desire to be your own contractor, you can find ways of doing it successfully. When you do not have enough time to educate yourself in the work or to manage the crews, however, you are better off hiring a professional general contractor to do the work for you. Even if you give up the hands-on profit and the supervision profit, you still are entitled to the investor profit.

Finding Fixer-Uppers with Outstanding Potential

Locating fixer-uppers with outstanding potential can take some time. Plenty of properties for sale fall into the fixer-upper category, but not all of them are worth buying. For example, you probably should stay away from a house with a faulty foundation. The cost of fixing a foundation generally is not recoverable in a new sales price. However, if you find a house that is structurally sound with only cosmetic blemishes, you may be on the trail of a great deal.

Be wary of any deal that looks too good. Always check out a fixer-upper thoroughly before you purchase it. This is fairly easy for someone with an extensive background in remodeling, but it can be a daunting task for the average investor. Professional building inspectors are available to take the burden off of your shoulders if you are not qualified to physically evaluate a property.

Assuming you don't have the ability to evaluate a building's structure and mechanical systems, make sure your purchase offer contains contingency clauses that will protect you if a professional inspection turns up negative information. Such clauses give you an escape from the purchase if a serious defect in the property is uncovered. Unless they have something to hide, most sellers will accept contingency contracts as long as the contracts establish a reasonable time for the contingencies to be removed. In other words, you might be given two weeks to have a property inspection performed and evaluated. If you like the report, you move ahead with the purchase. When a problem crops up, you can either walk away from the deal or renegotiate it to compensate for the defects discovered during the inspection. Contingency clauses protect you from buying an unknown building and tie up the property so that no one else can purchase it while you do your research.

We talked previously about buildings that can be changed from one use to another, such as a house that can be converted to professional office space or a duplex that can be expanded to house four rental units. Conversion projects often require substantial remodeling. This can be good if you plan to cash in on all of the elements of the job and as long as the market can bear the building's increased value and cost. Any property has some potential as a fixer-upper. Even the most opulent mansion in town can benefit from some type of improvement. Certain property types, however, offer the most reward for your effort—and a mansion probably isn't one of them.

Generally, you should avoid properties that have suffered structural damage. Refacing kitchen cabinets, replacing plumbing and light fixtures, and painting walls all can make sense from the perspective of a financial return. Fixing a cracked foundation, eliminating the cause of a leaking basement, or replacing a worn roof, however, probably will not produce much in the way of profits. For this reason, you must choose your jobs carefully. Look for properties that offer the best potential with the smallest amount of investment. More importantly, seek buildings that can benefit from improvements that historically have added value to real estate.

Financing Rundown Property

Finding financing for a fixer-upper can be difficult. Some lenders want nothing to do with rundown buildings in disrepair. Other lenders, however, are happy to provide both acquisition and improvement financing. When you find the right lender, you can buy buildings with almost no money down and even get paid for the work you do to improve the properties. The financing is very similar to the loan a homebuilder receives when buying a lot and building a house.

It's not unusual for a lender to simultaneously loan an investor money to acquire a property and establish a line of credit to fund improvements. If you haven't already initiated credit accounts with suppliers and subcontractors, you may need to use your own money in the short term. Lenders pay out the improvement money only after work is completed and inspected. This means you must find subcontractors and suppliers who will wait to be paid; otherwise, you will need some operating capital. Most subcontractors and suppliers are happy to wait for payment, however, if you prove to them that you have a loan in place that will pay them upon completion of the improvements.

I've worked with a lot of acquisition and improvement loans. One investor who comes to mind bought a single-family home for a very low price. He was able to obtain the acquisition loan without any down payment. The closing costs for the loan were rolled into the financing. Basically, he used none of his cash to buy the property. The investor did much of the work on the house himself and was able to pay himself for his labor out of the draws against the loan that he received from the lender. The finished house was worth a great deal more than it was when the investor bought it, and the profits had been earned with nearly no money out of pocket and a paycheck, of sorts, for the labor invested in the project.

If you don't have a track record as a remodeler or general contractor, you can run into resistance from lenders when you seek a fixer-upper deal. The solution to the problem is to engage either a construction manager or a general contractor to oversee the work for you. This will eat into your profits on the first few deals, but after awhile lenders should be willing to let you take the reins and run your own jobs. It's okay not to make all of your money on the first deal or two. Take your time, and build a reputation for yourself. Your patience will pay off in the future.

Many communities participate in different types of incentive programs, which often are funded by the government. Investors generally can find low-interest loans and even outright grants to improve their properties. Check your local department of housing development to see what funding is available in your area. Most of the programs are targeted for neighborhoods that have suffered and are hoping to rebound—perfect for the fixer-upper investor. If you have confidence in an area's revitalization program, take advantage of low purchase prices and attractive improvement loans and grants to create your own keepers. Assuming that the revitalization works, your buildings should escalate in value quickly and continue appreciating over the years to come.

Lining up financing for rehab projects may require you to knock on the doors of more lenders than a traditional purchase would. If you are committed to this field of real estate, however, your research will not be wasted. You will be able to approach the same lender time and again as you progress in your fixer-upper business. Do develop good relations with more than one lender, though. Loan officers tend to come and go rapidly. To avoid rejection if your favorite loan officer moves on, line up some other amicable lenders in advance.

Cost Overruns Ruin Projects

Builders, bankers, remodelers, and others in the real estate rehab business fear cost overruns—and for good reason. Cost overruns can ruin projects. When workers are assigned jobs on an hourly basis, it's easy for costs to escalate. If material prices are not locked in with solid quotes, sudden jumps in the market value of the materials can put a job in jeopardy. These are real and serious threats, but they are easy enough to avoid. By using contracts and quotes, you can control cost overruns nearly all of the time. It's not difficult, but it is vital to your projects.

Almost any reputable contractor will commit to a firm contract price for work that you request. A contractor insisting on hourly billing signals inexperience or warns that something is amiss. It's much better to work with written, conclusive contracts and contract prices than it is to agree to work on an hourly basis. Jobs performed on a time and material (T&M) basis can easily generate costs that are much higher than you expected when you signed on with the contractor.

Material costs can skyrocket in a short period of time. I've seen jobs start with moderate lumber prices, only to have the prices jump outrageously in just a few weeks. To avoid this problem, you must work with material suppliers who lock in their prices for set periods of time. It used to be easy to get a price quote and lock-in for at least 30 days. Nowadays, though, it can be difficult to get a price lock for even one week. This is not the case with all suppliers. Contractors who buy regularly from the same suppliers often can get longer locks. For example, my lumber supplier will lock in prices on a per-job basis, even when I'm building a new house. Once you become established in the field, you probably will be able to get longer locks.

If you hire a general contractor to handle all aspects of your job, it's not necessary for you to establish relationships with suppliers. Your agreement with the general contractor will encompass the total job. It's then up to the contractor to lock in the subcontractors and suppliers.

Selling in the Dust

When you work with fixer-uppers, you can wait until you finish improving them, or you can try selling or renting them in the dust of remodeling. The latter may shorten a building's time on the market, but not everyone has the vision to look beyond a gutted structure and see a dream home. If the kitchen is without cabinets and counters and the bathrooms are without fixtures, the property may be a tough sell. As long as the property basics are in good shape, though, you may be able to presell or prerent without a lot of trouble. Personally, I wait for a job to be finished and cleaned before I show it.

Fixer-uppers may be the pot of gold at the end of your rainbow. Although get-rich-quick schemes usually don't work, it is very possible to make huge amounts of money in a short time when you become proficient in working with fixer-uppers. My personal experience with rehab projects has been extremely good, so I'm biased, but I do believe that rehab and conversion projects are the most profitable deals investors can undertake on a regular basis.

As strong as the income can be from fixer-uppers, it pales in comparison with the potential money to be made with conversion properties. Conversion work often requires remodeling, but if you can couple it with renovations at the same time, the profit margin can be tremendous. To learn more about conversion properties, let's turn to the next chapter.

CHAPTER 14

Making Money with Conversion Properties

When it comes to making money in real estate, few opportunities offer as much potential as conversion properties. Whenever you find real estate that you can convert from one use to a higher and better use, you're on to something. For example, a home that can be modified into a triplex would make a good deal. Fixer-uppers offer tremendous potential, but conversion properties are even better. It's entirely possible to make tens of thousands of dollars in less than three months with a strong conversion property. What's the catch? Prime conversion properties usually are not easy to find at affordable prices. But for those people willing to invest their time searching for them, conversion properties can be like buried treasures. You can even make money with conversion properties without buying them. That's right. If you use purchase options right and set them up with assignment clauses, you can gain control of properties, change their zoning usage, and sell them for a handsome profit without ever actually owning them.

Conversion projects can be houses, apartment buildings, motels, retail space, or other types of real estate. Even raw land can qualify as a conversion project, although it is especially risky. Sellers usually don't advertise their properties as conversion projects, largely because the sellers don't know that they're sitting on gold mines. It's like going to a yard sale and finding a valuable antique that someone is selling as junk. Without a doubt, the market offers some glorious opportunities, but you have to recognize them when you see them. Plus, you should not limit yourself to properties listed for sale. Some of the best deals are made when investors contact property owners directly and ask whether the owners might consider selling their properties.

Looking beneath the Surface

The key to working with conversion properties is being able to look beneath the surface. If a property's potential is obvious, either the property will not be on the market or it will sell at a premium price. To make big money, you must uncover properties with conversion potential, buy them as they are, change them to what they can be, then cash in with sales. All this may seem difficult, but it's not. It is labor intensive, though. You will have to work for what you get, and you will run into a lot of deadends. Many of the properties you research will not have the potential you seek. When you find a great property, the owner may not be willing to sell. Be prepared to experience a lot of lost time and disappointment, but know that when you do score, the money can be significant.

You don't have to be a magician to make money with conversions. You do, however, have to be creative, have a vision for the future, and have enough time to do extensive research. Time spent in research is your best investment when it comes to conversion properties. It is the research that gives you the edge, the knowledge, and the power to win at your real estate game.

You can find a wide variety of conversion projects when you dig deeply enough. Perhaps a single-family house can be converted to professional office space. You might find an apartment building that can be adapted to co-op or condo status. Buying an old motel and converting it into condos can work. Converting a mixed-use building to all retail space can pay off well. Tearing down an existing building can give you a lot that you can use for an expensive commercial venture. You might turn excess farmland into country estates for a subdivision. You might convert a large house to multifamily use. A discarded church could be modified for commercial uses. The possibilities for conversions are endless.

Investors take advantage of conversion properties by looking beneath the surface. Uncovering a four-unit building that has been boarded up might not seem like much of a find; however, if you learned that the vacant building was taken for taxes and that it could be converted to medical office space, you could be on the verge of unearthing a little buried treasure. Rehabbing a four-unit building might prove profitable, but rehabbing the same building while changing its use could produce powerful returns. If you don't want to get your hands dirty, you can hire people to do the work and still profit from your research. You could even option or purchase the property in its present condition, then sell it to a rehabber for a nice profit without ever doing anything to the building, other than defining its potential. You have to find the diamonds in the rough before you can polish them for sale, though.

Do Your Homework

If you want to make money on conversion projects, you must do your homework. Think of yourself as a prospector in search of buried treasure. You know the treasure exists, but you don't know exactly where to find it or how to take control of it. It's best if you can identify conversion properties yourself, but you also can use the assistance of specialized buyers' brokers, who concentrate on working with investors. If you get a really good broker, the broker can bring deals to you. However, don't sit around waiting for the broker to call. Double your efforts by conducting your own search. Nobody has more interest in your financial status than you do.

When looking for your winning conversion property, your work probably will start at the local offices of the municipality in which your potential property is located. The zoning requirements likely will be the first consideration. A trip to the tax office to confirm existing tax value should be on your agenda. Then settle down with old newspaper files at the local library or with a real estate broker's Multiple Listing Service books. You also might set up a consultation with a real estate appraiser. Your goal is to collect as much information about the building as possible from as many justifiable sources as possible. Once you have the data, you can design your game plan.

Buying property without quantifiable information usually is a major mistake. You should spend the time required to gather as much information as possible before making an offer to purchase real estate. Much of your research will cost you nothing more than your time. Other elements of your research, however, might come with a steep price tag. For example, hiring an engineering and surveying firm to provide you with development reports can be very expensive. You might spend several thousand dollars just to find out that your project will fail. If you do, consider yourself lucky. Just think of the money you might have lost without the reports. Paying for information that you don't want to hear is bad. Failing to obtain the information and learning the hard way is even worse.

Before you buy a conversion property, you must define all elements of your plan. This can encompass anything from zoning changes to local rental rates. The information you seek varies depending on the type of property you want to acquire. Don't stop digging until you have all of the answers you need. A few sample questions follow:

- What are local rental rates?
- At what prices have comparable properties been selling?
- Does the spread between the purchase price, the cost of alterations needed, and the probable sales price justify the purchase?
- What is the historical sales time required to sell the type of property you are creating?
- Do you have enough cash to carry the deal until it sells?
- Could you survive financially if the property doesn't sell as quickly as you wish?

Having the Vision to See a Project Through

Having the vision to spot strong conversion properties, then following up with research, is only part of what you will need to win at the conversion game. You also will require some financial clout and the ability to complete what you start. The financial clout can be—and should be—arranged in advance. Seek out lenders that will work with you on a conversion property before you find the property. Go shopping only after you have your lenders in place. This will save you time and frustration and make your purchase offers more viable to sellers.

We've talked about how to see conversion properties for their potential. Talking to lenders puts you in a position to act quickly once you have found a suitable property. However, you still need the ability to complete the conversion. Maybe you will do the work yourself. If not, line up your contractors in advance. You may need to hunt for only general contractors, or you might have to find suppliers and subcontractors—a much bigger job. Whichever the case, accomplish it early in the process, before you have a job to do. Not only will you have your workers on standby, the workers may alert you to conversion deals.

It's not uncommon for workers to partner with investors in joint ventures. In fact, I started out as a worker teamed up with an accountant. Many sellers pay remodelers to spruce up their properties before the sellers put them on the market; therefore, remodelers often know of potential properties before brokers. Once you have your network of contractors in place, their scouting efforts may alert you to a number of good opportunities. If the remodelers know you will hire them for conversion work, they will be motivated to make you aware of potential deals.

Sell It or Lease It?

Once you plan to buy a conversion project, you must decide whether you will lease it for rental income or sell it for a quick profit. With conversion projects, either tactic usually works. The cash flow from a lease on a conversion project can be quite good. Of course, it all depends on the acquisition cost, the cost of improvements, and what the current market will bear in rental rates. Real estate never offers guarantees, but conversion projects generally have excellent potential as both quick-flips and long-term rental properties. This is part of what makes the projects so attractive to investors.

If you sell your building quickly, the tax bite can hurt. Depending on your tax bracket and status, you could surrender a lot of cash to Uncle Sam. Keeping the building for a few years may make a sale much more profitable. Your tax experts can help you in this matter. On the other hand, leasing a building out can yield tax advantages and a steady income. Both tactics can work, depending on your goals as an investor. If you are playing the market for retirement, leasing out conversion projects can be ideal. Selling conversion projects can earn you some quick cash and allow you to move onto other projects, if that's your goal. Buying right, keeping a han-

dle on improvement costs, and having a solid plan for your end result make the most out of any conversion project.

Selling a conversion project can be quite easy. In fact, it's likely
that you could have the property under contract for a quick sale before
the conversion work is finished. To illustrate, let's look at an example.

For Example . . .

Assume that you find a duplex that is zoned for four
units and that has enough square footage to accommodate the
additional units. Your major work will be on the building's interior. Kitchens and bathrooms must be added; new doors are
needed; and of course partition walls must be built. Let's say
that you buy the property, obtain the permit for four units, and
start your conversion work. As soon as you have the permit in
hand, you can begin to advertise the property for sale.

Because small multifamily buildings are very popular, it
should be easy to generate interest in your project. Prospective
buyers will have to possess some vision to see through the remodeling chaos and to envision your plans for the finished project.
Good investors have no trouble doing this. If you have all of
your marketing ducks in a row, it's very possible that you could
see purchase offers in just a week or two. It might take two
months to complete the conversion work, but by then you could
have the building under contract for a quick sale. In some cases,
your buyer might already be approved for a loan and waiting
for an appraisal on the finished project. As soon as the remodeling is completed, you can get an appraisal to confirm the anticipated value and close your deal. It's a nice way to do business. ■

Selling a project while it is under construction reduces the
amount of time that you must carry the cost of holding the building.

This allows you to either sell at a lower price or to pocket more profits at the time of sale. Some investors prefer to wait for a finished product before putting the building on the market, however.

Just as you can sell in advance, you should be able to prelease your building. Offer prospective tenants a special price due to the remodeling. Explain that prices will go up after completion, due to the increased carrying cost. Most professionals understand and accept this concept. Having your tenants lined up in advance reduces your out-of-pocket expenses once the building is completed. In the worst case, you will not get advance tenants and will have to wait for completion. However, for every tenant you sign in advance, you save money. Plus, if you rent out the building in advance, each new tenant provides security and credibility for the next prospective tenant.

The sell or lease decision is totally personal, depending on your game plan. As a backup strategy to selling, however, consider leasing out your project for a year or so if the sales market sags. Rather than take a loss due to the sluggish market, collect rent until the market regains financial ground. It's common for rental demand to be higher than buying demand, but you can win both ways with the right conversion projects.

One of the Biggest Money Makers

Conversions probably are one of the largest money makers available to average investors. You can buy into a conversion deal with limited cash and usually can finance most of the project, including the conversion costs. The ability to flip conversion projects quickly for hefty profits makes them extremely desirable. Accepting a certain level of risk is necessary, but advance planning greatly reduces the gamble. Given enough research, you can almost ensure yourself a profit. Lenders that work with conversions are well aware of their relative safety; however, lenders are most comfortable dealing with experienced conversion investors. If you are embarking on your first project, you might do well to team up with an experienced general contractor. Expect lenders to request a detailed proposal from you on your plans to profit from your project.

The prepurchase work required for a conversion project—appraisals, zoning verifications, code compliance checks—is more complex than it is for a standard purchase. Because lenders must predict future value with before-and-after appraisals, they may be a bit conservative. Anyone putting up money for a conversion is likely to want the security of knowing that the people involved in the project will see it through and complete the job on time and on budget. Plus, an end result must be detailed. This means that you must show a marketing plan for either selling or leasing the property.

In some conversion projects, remodeling is not the key element involved. For example, if I were to take a tract of land and rezone it for a higher and better use, I would have no remodeling to do. This is not to say that I would not incur conversion expenses. The restructuring program would involve survey costs, as well as fees paid to engineers, attorneys, and others involved in the program. If the project has enough potential, a lender probably will bankroll the deal. You can, in many cases, get through conversion projects without spending much of your own money. The creative strategy you put into a conversion project is often the most important part of your investment.

The Best Quick-Flips

The best quick-flips are usually conversion deals. The reason is simple: Because conversion properties generally are much more valuable as soon as the conversions are completed, they can make astounding amounts of money quickly. Traditional real estate investors often look for a good rate of return on their investments. When the rate is twice what they would earn in cash investments, the investors are more than happy. You might well imagine how pleased investors are when they make ten times the return or more with conversion properties. Can this really be possible? Let me give you an example.

For Example . . .

We don't need to juggle a lot of figures to see the value of investing in conversion properties. Assume that you make a down payment of $40,000 to acquire a property. The down payment might be your cash, equity you have in other properties, or a note the seller holds. You borrow and invest another $50,000 in the property over a period of 90 days. Then you sell the property for a full profit, after brokerage fees and closings costs, of $60,000. To summarize, you invested $40,000 for three months, and it might have been borrowed money to begin with. After selling the property, you regained all of the money invested and saw a profit of $60,000—not a bad return, by anyone's standards. ∎

The possibilities for high rates of return with conversion properties are the stuff that dreams are made of. You can realize the dream if you work hard enough. As you learn the ropes—and you can earn while you learn—the eventual rewards may be more than you ever imagined.

CHAPTER 15

Cost-Effective Building Improvements

Cost-effective building improvements can prove profitable for real estate investors whether they sell a building or rent it out. The right improvements make a property more desirable and, therefore, more profitable. Historically, some investments generate much greater returns than others. For example, the best place to sink your improvement money in a single-family home is in kitchen remodeling, followed by bathroom remodeling. Adding a deck or a garage also can make a house more profitable. Other types of improvements, however, such as replacing carpeting or drapes in residential properties, may not make financial sense. Investors who work with retail or office space have other considerations when it comes to making improvements.

Knowing how to assess an improvement's value is instrumental in making money. Sometimes it's best not to make any improvements. For example, if you buy an office building with acceptable carpeting, you probably should not upgrade it. Other times, putting money into a building can make the property much more valuable. For instance, improving an office building's aura might attract first-class professional tenants, or creating a warm environment for residents can make an apartment building much easier to rent to the best tenants for the highest prices.

Increasing the Return on an Investment

You may be able to increase the return on an investment by improving the property. The question is whether the improvement adds to your investment. Some investors have an eye for improvement projects, but most depend on professional appraisers to determine when an improvement is worthwhile. Even with my experience in construction and remodeling, I use appraisers when deciding whether to fund building improvements. I would feel very vulnerable without the appraisal reports I commission. You, too, should consult with appraisers before making major improvement investments.

I break down real estate improvements into two main categories. The first category includes improvements made to enhance a property's sales price. The second category comprises improvements used to attract tenants. Sometimes improvements fall into both categories. For example, remodeling the kitchens in an apartment building might both increase its sales value and draw more tenants. Improvements that span both categories are, of course, the most desirable improvements to make.

If you invest in improvements designed to pull in more tenants, attract better quality tenants, or increase rents, you must weigh the amount of time required to regain the cost of the improvements. When you make investments for sales value, you may not realize the return on the investments until you sell the property—and you might not see it then. Ideally, concentrate on improvements that can boost tenant appeal and sales value at the same time.

Defining the Term

What constitutes an improvement? For our purposes, I use the word *improvement* to mean an enhancement meant to increase property value. Even this definition is confusing, though. Painting a rental unit, for example, is a necessary evil. Although the improvement normally does not increase a property's value, it can make a unit easier to rent. Considering the relatively low cost of painting, the improvement makes sense in most situations. Can the same be said for replacing all of the carpeting in a house? Not usually. Carpet replacement will not increase the value of a house enough to cover the cost of the work. Carpet replacement should be considered maintenance rather than an improvement. (Maintenance preserves a structure's quality.) Installing a new roof could be viewed as an improvement, but I see it as maintenance. It's something that must be done regularly, but it doesn't raise a property's value substantially. The line between maintenance and improvement sometimes is difficult to distinguish, and improvements are sometimes invaluable even if they don't increase property value. Confusing, I know, so let me explain.

Installing a new heating system in a building is an improvement, but it likely will not produce a full return on the cost when the property is sold. In fact, most improvements and maintenance costs cannot be recovered fully. Only a few types of improvements produce profits during a sale. Improvements can draw a sale quicker, however, which can save an investor money in carrying costs. Therefore, it is possible for improvements to make money indirectly.

Maintenance also can stimulate a quicker sale. If an investor replaces an antiquated heating system with a new, energy-efficient model, for instance, a prospective buyer might purchase the building more quickly—or even pay more for the property. Although the investor probably would not recover the total cost of the heating system, the work may prove valuable. If fact, money saved in reduced interest cost for carrying the building during the sales process could offset the loss.

Maintenance Is Not the Same as Improvement

I've said it before, and I'll say it again: Maintenance is not the same as improvement. I cover maintenance in this chapter because the two are so easily confused.

Landlords typically factor in a cost for routine maintenance by computing a percentage of their gross rental income to cover expected costs. Ten percent of gross income is a typical figure used in spreadsheet calculations. Of course, the amount may not be enough, or it may be too much.

The money set aside for routine maintenance might cover the replacement of light bulbs, the occasional clearing of drains that become clogged, and the cutting of lawns. Rarely does the maintenance budget build in enough money to cover large expenses, such as a new roof, a new heating system, or major plumbing problems. These big-ticket items often are unexpected when they occur.

Smart investors maintain a good amount of money in their operational funds because they know that borrowing cash to cover maintenance costs is not a good practice. The act of maintaining a building doesn't justify a rental increase and rarely creates additional cash value. For these reasons, the money spent on maintenance is hard to recover. When you buy a building, inspect it or have it inspected thoroughly, and plan for major repairs, as well as routine maintenance. In other words, expect the unexpected, and budget money to cover crises when you are projecting your cash flow numbers.

When You Make the Wrong Improvements

The wrong improvements can cost more than the money you invest in them. Many people have spent hard-earned money to improve a property, only to see their cash buried in the building. I have known several investors who have stumbled into major investments that produced losses when the properties were sold. This doesn't have to happen to you. With the right research, you can avoid most of the problems associated with poor investment decisions. Let's look at an example that illustrates the point.

For Example . . .

Assume that you purchase a duplex in fair condition. You would like to make a lot of improvements to it, but your money is limited. To start, let's say that the duplex's wood siding is old and in need of fresh paint. You consider covering the duplex with vinyl siding so that it will be maintenance-free in years to come. Vinyl siding is an improvement that might produce a reasonable return on the investment, but this depends on many factors. If your duplex is the only one in the neighborhood that doesn't have maintenance-free siding, you might be well served to make the capital improvement. However, if your duplex will be one of a few in the area with vinyl siding, your decision is more complicated. If you plan to keep the building for a long time, having a maintenance-free exterior could be comforting. However, if you plan to sell in the next few years, you probably would be much better off to simply paint the existing siding, assuming that it is in good repair. This type of comparison work is required to make wise decisions.

Now let's say that the duplex contains old electrical wiring. Though the wiring is safe enough, you want to upgrade the electrical service and rewire the building. This improvement makes financial sense if you will keep the building for a long time and can afford to make the improvement without much of a return. Tenants rarely pay more for a unit with new wiring—especially if the old wiring was safe. An appraiser will give a little extra value for the modern wiring, but not nearly enough to pay for its cost of installation. You must make this type of improvement because you want to, not because it's profitable. ∎

Smart improvements can be almost anything, but they usually add both desirability and value to a property. For example, installing built-in dishwashers in your apartments could be considered a dual-benefit improvement. The dishwashers should increase the building's value, as well as attract more tenants. This doesn't mean that the value of your building will escalate in an amount equal to the money you spent on the dishwashers, but some of the investment should be matched in appraised value. The same type of situation could occur if you refinish the kitchen cabinets in your apartments. However, installing designer hardware on the doors, windows, and cabinets normally would not fill both needs. It might influence some tenants, but it probably would not increase the property value.

You have many ways to determine which improvements fall into the "smart" category. The most reliable is to have before-and-after appraisals performed on your property before you make the improvements. Talking to lenders also can be quite enlightening. Most lenders willing to make improvement loans have a better-than-average awareness of which improvements are financially feasible. Real estate brokers also can help you assess potential improvements; however, not all brokers are savvy in terms of return on improvements, and some brokers may tell you what you want to hear in hopes of getting your business in the future. Ideally, talk to some investors who draw from first-hand experience. While you may be their competitor, you might find it mutually beneficial to share thoughts. In the end, evaluate the opinions you have obtained, but give the most weight to the professional appraiser's assessment.

Special Improvement Programs

Special improvement programs vary greatly in their intended uses. Some of the programs offer low-interest loans. Others dispense outright grants that need not be repaid. Others match the funds you put into a building for improvements. Most of the programs originate with the federal government, but are administered locally. You can refer to government publications to see specifically what types of programs currently are being offered, but you need to check with your local municipality for programs available in your area. Start with the community development office or the housing development office. If need be, check with the local code enforcement office. Generally, the people who work for your town or city will be quite helpful in providing information on funding programs.

I have helped many investors find improvement programs that fit their needs. In some cases, the investors received large blocks of money as grants for community revitalization. Although the investors were required to sink the money into their properties, they didn't have to pay back the grants. A number of other investors benefitted from low-interest loans. Some of the programs required the investors to improve their properties and to maintain ownership of the buildings for at least five years. If the investors met the criteria, they didn't have to repay the money. These programs change from time to time, so consult with local community development offices regularly.

Undertaking Cosmetic Improvements

Cosmetic improvements make a property look better, but have no effect on structural elements. They are not necessary improvements, even if they enhance a property's value. Some people think of cosmetic improvements as inexpensive ways to dress up a building—and they can be. However, some cosmetic work is quite expensive. Examples of costly cosmetic improvements include new siding, carpeting, floor or wall tile, kitchen cabinets, and so forth. Know what you're getting into when you decide to make cosmetic improvements.

Structural repairs rarely add value to a property because appraisers expect buildings to be structurally sound. If a property lacks structural integrity, it should be fixed to meet standard market value. The money invested, however, will not yield much of a profit percentage. Cosmetic improvements, on the other hand, can add value to a building. With the right plan, a little money can go a long way in making a building more desirable. The cosmetic improvements undertaken depend heavily on the type of building being improved. For example, a single-family home might benefit greatly from a stenciled border around the kitchen walls. This type of work could make the house more desirable and, therefore, more profitable. The best cosmetic improvement in an office building might be adding potted plants in the reception area. Both of these improvements are minor, but they can have a strong impact on people's reaction to the properties. Sometimes creating a comfortable environment, that is, a property's desirability, is worth more than a cash increase in value.

All sorts of cosmetic improvements can be undertaken on all types of buildings. Shopping centers, office buildings, houses, apartments, and other structures all can benefit from cosmetic improvements. If you plan to make cosmetic improvements, make sure of your motivation before doing so. Are you doing the work to increase your property's cash value? Will you tackle the improvements to attract tenants? Is it your intention that the improvements will make your property sell faster, although not necessarily for a higher price? Once you have answered these types of questions honestly, you can evaluate the cost and feasibility of doing the work.

Major Remodeling Can Be Risky

Major remodeling can create strong equity in a building, but it also can be very risky. Investors who commit to big remodeling jobs can spend tens of thousands of dollars without seeing much return on their investments. Conversion projects typically require substantial remodeling. This is to be expected, and the remodeling is factored into an overall project. Not all investors think of major remodeling, however, when they buy a typical apartment building or house. When an investor does not plan the remodeling before purchasing a property, the cost of the remodeling can turn a profitable building into a cash sinkhole.

The decision to remodel should be made with a business head. If you allow yourself to get emotionally involved in the process, you set yourself up for financial failure. Some investors get caught up in the excitement of remodeling and just don't know when to stop. For example, an investor may have a kitchen floor replaced and like the results so much that he decides to replace all of the flooring. For this reason, you must stay focused and make decisions wisely when remodeling your buildings.

In residential properties, kitchen and bathroom remodeling are the two most popular and the two most profitable forms of remodeling. Even so, the work may not be justified. If you own a house that you use for rental property, for example, installing a new kitchen could be unwise if it will take a long time to recover the cost through increased rents. Assuming the kitchen is not too outdated or rundown, you probably should leave it alone. On the other hand, if you are getting ready to sell the house, remodeling the kitchen might make good sense. You must weigh the circumstances in each situation.

Landlords who read magazine articles touting certain remodeling jobs as good investments can get themselves in trouble. Rental properties cannot be compared to primary residences. The investor who adds a fancy chair rail in the dining room of a rental property, for instance, might be shocked to find that the tenant's children tack up their artwork on the molding. Experienced landlords try to stay away from improvements that can be defaced or worn out quickly.

Hire an Appraiser

If you are contemplating a major building improvement or remodeling, hire a professional appraiser to do a before-and-after appraisal or to work with you as a consultant. I have used appraisers in both capacities. For example, an appraiser functioning as a consultant could answer your question: how much does a two-car garage add to the value of a home? Getting the answer to a single query is much less expensive than commissioning a full-blown appraisal. The information you receive is not always as accurate, but it usually comes close enough to work with. Money spent on appraisers is almost always money well spent.

The decision to improve a property is one that must be addressed financially. Confine your thoughts to business, and don't get caught up in doing things you always wished you could do, such as installing a hot tub in a gazebo. Stick to improvements that will pay for themselves in one way or another. This way, your experience with remodeling and improvements will be much happier.

CHAPTER 16

Building Relationships with Real Estate Brokers

Some investors rely on their own abilities to buy and sell real estate, but far more depend on brokers. Real estate brokers have much to offer investors. Most brokers are part of a Multiple Listing Service (MLS), which gives them instant access to properties for sale, buildings that have sold recently, and other valuable information pertaining to the current real estate market. Much of the information is available to the general public, but it's much more difficult to find and use when you must seek it out piece by piece. Multiple Listing Services compile the information and make it readily available to MLS participants. The ability to sit down with brokers and look through their MLS books is a great advantage to anyone seeking to buy or sell real estate.

Licensing requirements for real estate agents and brokers can be very stringent. In almost all cases, some form of education is required, and licensees typically must pass a written test before becoming licensed. Many states require licensees to participate in continuing education programs to maintain their licenses. A lot of brokers volunteer to take additional courses for specialized training. Members of the National Association of REALTORS® attend special courses to obtain the REALTOR® designation. Since real estate is a complex business, it's important for a licensee to strive for as much quality education as possible. Considering the study that brokers often do, they are normally much better qualified when it comes to real estate issues than an average investor is.

Two types of brokers exist. Some brokers work for the sellers of real estate in the traditional brokerage role. If you have property to sell, this is the type of broker you should work with. If you are buying real estate, however, you might consider using a buyer's broker. We will discuss the distinctions between the two types of brokers later in this chapter.

Should You Work with a Broker?

It's probably safe to say that you should work with a broker when buying or selling real estate. Because most people don't completely understand real estate and the laws governing it, it's difficult for them to perform well without some guidance. Some investors do represent themselves, and some of them do it very well. Most people, however, need help. You might think you can get by without a broker if you retain a good real estate attorney to answer your legal questions. Of course, it's always good business to work with an attorney by your side; however, they usually are not qualified real estate salespeople.

Good brokers fulfill many roles for an investor. Some tasks they perform are obvious; others are not. The public perception of brokers and the principles they apply in the real estate business often is clouded. People just don't know what really goes on behind the scenes. Being a broker and a brokerage owner, I can clear up any misunderstandings.

Brokers list buildings to sell. This puts them in the business of helping owners sell their properties. Brokerages advertise properties for sale in hopes of attracting buyers. When buyers respond to the ads, the brokers work with the buyers to help them find and acquire suitable properties. Therefore, a broker's basic duties consist of offering properties for sale as a representative of the sellers and helping buyers find real estate to purchase. Most people know all this. In addition to these obvious roles, good brokers do much more. An experienced broker can help a buyer find financing, track the closing process and keep it on track, and work with property inspectors, among other things. Brokers also can provide valuable research to help investors plan strategies for their investment properties. Brokers can do a lot to help you in your career as a real estate investor.

A broker generally earns his money only when he procures a closed sale. Payment for services rendered usually comes in the form of a percentage of the sales price. Some sellers resent paying commissions for sales they feel they could make themselves. Real estate agents work hard for their money, though. Brokerages usually write and pay for all advertising to attract buyers. Brokers spend hours showing properties that don't sell, which means they spend a lot of time working without getting paid for their efforts. Earning commissions on sales that do close helps balance all the "unpaid" hours a broker puts in on unsold properties.

Some people think that the anticipated commission amount is added on to the sales price. But usually, a building being financed can't be sold for more than its appraised value. The commission comes out of the sales price and is normally not an add-on. In some cases, a seller might be willing to sell for less if a commission is not being paid, but an appraisal will determine the value of the property. If you are a seller and feel the commission is not costing you anything, you're wrong. On the other hand, if you think that an agent is getting rich from the commission, you are probably still wrong. The bottom line: If you are happy with the deal and the money you earn, you shouldn't resent the broker's commission.

Seller's Broker vs. Buyer's Broker

What's the difference between a seller's broker and a buyer's broker? A seller's broker works *for* the seller and *with* the buyer. This means that the broker's loyalty is to the seller, not the buyer. Law requires the broker to treat the buyer fairly and honestly, but the broker is not required to disclose everything she knows about the seller's position. For example, if you make an offer to buy a property and tell the broker that you want to offer $150,000, but that you will go as high as $165,000, the broker is obligated to share your conversation with the seller. On the other hand, if the seller counters with an offer of $160,000, but tells the broker that your counter of $155,000 will be acceptable, the broker doesn't have to share this information with you.

A buyer's broker works *for* the buyer and *with* the seller. Essentially, the roles described in the paragraph above are reversed. Technically, a person can act as both a buyer's broker and a seller's broker, although not on the same transaction. In reality, most good buyers' brokers don't list properties. This means that the brokers have more time to search for the types of properties their clients want to buy because they don't have to solicit listings.

Many people think the buyer must pay the buyer's broker directly. This is not true. Buyers' brokers can be paid by buyers or sellers. Most sellers' brokerages that cobroke—that is, work with other brokerages and split commissions—are willing to share commissions with buyers' brokers. It is not unusual for a buyer to pay a buyer's broker directly, but no law requires the buyer to foot the bill.

Not all brokerages (or brokers) are alike. The obvious difference, as we've just discussed, is that some brokerages are sellers' brokerages and some are buyers' brokerages. Other differences exist, however. For example, some brokerages specialize in commercial properties, working only with shopping centers. Other brokerages handle apartment buildings or houses. Finding brokerages that specialize in your property type is a definite advantage.

It stands to reason that if a person does the same type of work day in and day out, she should be good at what she does. As an investor, you need to build a list of qualified professionals you can work with and depend on. This includes appraisers, lawyers, lenders, and brokers, not to mention the many other professionals you may require for various types of real estate.

Role of Real Estate Brokers

What is the role of a real estate broker? We've already hit on the highlights. In the most simple terms, brokers are paid to arrange the sales of real estate. The expanded version of a broker's role can include anything from playing taxi driver to taking a cake out of the oven. (The aroma of fresh baked food can help sell a house, so some brokers have their sellers put something in the oven before a showing.) In fact, good brokers provide numerous services for their customers and clients.

The job may start with a listing. Getting listings of properties to sell is a role of a seller's broker, but not all seller's brokers pursue listings. It's fairly common for some agents to be listing agents while others are selling agents. This doesn't mean that either type of broker is a buyer's broker. Are you confused yet?

Some real estate professionals are much more comfortable listing properties than they are selling them. (I am just the opposite.) Because most agents work on a cobroke basis, a listing broker gets paid even when another broker makes the sale. Sometimes the best listing brokers have deep community roots and a lot of friends and contacts. Visibility within the community helps when seeking listings. Selling brokers don't need to know a lot of people to make money. A selling broker can run ads in newspapers, then field calls to make sales.

When a broker helps a buyer find a property, it's common practice for the broker to work with the buyer to structure an offer to purchase. The selling agent then delivers the offer to the listing agent (or to the owner if the selling agent is also the listing agent). The listing agent presents the purchase offer to the seller and explains the contractual agreement. Either or both parties to the deal may make counteroffers. Once a deal is struck, the selling broker might help the buyer coordinate property inspections. The listing broker likely will work with an appraiser during the closing process. Both brokers should stay on top of all closing procedures to make sure that everything progresses smoothly and in a timely fashion.

A lot of selling brokers assist buyers in finding financing sources. When paperwork must get from one place to another, either the listing broker or the selling broker usually takes care of it. Brokers often must act as sounding boards for buyers during the closing process. Many times, buyers get cold feet, or what's called buyer's remorse. It is up to the selling broker to keep the buyers motivated and happy during the closing process, which can take anywhere from about two weeks to as long as six weeks or more. When the time comes to close a deal, both brokers normally attend the closing to answer questions either the buyer or seller may have. Plus, brokers like to be on hand to pick up their commission checks when a deal is done.

Not all brokers invest their time in a sale's follow-up work. They feel that once a contract is signed and delivered, the deal is in the hands of others. These brokers often lose sales that could have been saved during the closing process. As an investor, you should find brokers willing to put in the extra effort to hold your deals together. When you interview brokers, start by asking them to describe their normal procedures during the process of a sale and closing. Your experience with a particular broker, however, will be the best proof of the broker's job performance. Because investors often buy multiple properties over time, they have the opportunity to test different brokers until they find ones they like working with.

Hooking up with the Right Brokers

Having the right brokers by your side can mean the difference between getting average deals and getting superior deals—especially when your relationships land you on the brokers' networks of investors. It's common for brokers to offer new listings to their networks of investors before placing public advertising. Some brokers also scan new MLS listings on a weekly basis and bring suitable properties to the attention of the right investors. This arrangement works well for the brokers themselves, as well as for sellers and buyers. The brokers save money on advertising and get quick sales. Sellers, too, realize fast sales, and investors get great offerings early in the marketing process.

You can hook up with the right brokers in many ways. One very effective way is to create a brochure for yourself. Not many investors do this, but the ones who do get noticed. If you are serious about buying investment property, take the time to create a winning sales piece of your own. It doesn't have to be expensive. A simple letter is all you really need, but a nice tri-fold brochure is better. Use your space in the piece to tell brokers and sellers who you are, what you do (invest in real estate), the types of properties you are interested in, and any other special details you might have to offer (for example, you have an established line of credit and can close quickly on properties). Once people in the business know you are a serious investor, you probably will get a number of special opportunities.

You can hand-deliver your promotional pieces to suitable real estate brokerages. If you want to buy property in a particular neighborhood, go door to door and leave your brochures for property owners to review. You never know when an owner is about to list a property for sale, and if you can get to the seller before she lists, you might get a better price.

Once you find the right brokers, you can be faced with more business than you can handle. You might be presented with several potential properties each week. This can be overwhelming and quite confusing, but don't get too caught up in the excitement. Sort through the properties carefully, and weigh your criteria. Experienced investment brokers can produce a lot of viable deals in a short period of time. Don't feel pressured to act on all of the offerings.

You can cut down on the bombardment of offerings if they become too much for you by refining your criteria and requiring brokers to adhere to your rules. Any good broker will respect your wishes. For example, if you only want to see buildings with four to eight rental units with price ranges of $150,000 to $400,000, say so. If you require a positive cash flow, let it be known. Define your needs tightly if you are getting more paperwork than you can handle.

Assuming that you are buying property, I strongly suggest that you develop good relationships with experienced, specialized buyers' brokers. Seasoned brokers will not try to force-feed you buildings that don't fit the profile you set forth. This is not to say that you will not get an occasional offering for a stray property, but these opportunities can be well worth your time to investigate. Professional brokers who take their work seriously normally do not waste a buyer's time with dud properties.

Buying from a Seller's Broker

Buying from a seller's broker can work out, but as a buyer, you're better off with a buyer's broker. Until fairly recently, buyers' brokers had no formal roles. Traditionally, all brokers were sellers' brokers—and most buyers continue to use them. Some aspects of buying from a seller's broker can be risky, however, if you don't know the rules of the road.

When you deal with a traditional broker who represents a seller, but works with you, be careful what you say—the broker may be obligated to repeat it to the seller. Sellers' brokers are required by law to be honest with buyers and to treat them fairly, but the fiduciary relationship (loyalty) is between the seller and the broker. This puts the buyer at some disadvantage if he discloses too much information to the broker. In other words, don't say anything to the broker that you would not want the seller to hear.

The Reality of a Purchase

Some investors feel that they need not invest personal time following through on a deal when they have a broker to do it for them. In reality, you may be the only person who can pull your deal through. It's like a landlord who hires a management company to run her building. The management company is supposed to take care of day-to-day management duties, but without the landlord to oversee the management company the property may suffer. The same is true with brokers. Making arrangements for broker representation is not the end of the story.

If you work with a really good broker, your duties in the course of a sale will be minimal. However, if you are unfortunate enough to land a broker who is not so good, you may be the only person who cares whether your deal succeeds. It is in your best interest to study real estate principles and practices and learn what goes on at every step of a transaction. Dearborn, the publisher of this book, offers a long line of books for consumers and professionals that can educate you in specific areas of real estate. Possessing this professional knowledge is a great advantage as you manage your brokers and your business.

Many investors accept information about a property at face value. In reality, you may have to dig a lot deeper than the sales hype presented to you. Brokers and sellers sometimes embellish their offerings. While fraud, lack of disclosure, and deceit are illegal and uncommon when dealing with reputable brokers, puffing is not so rare. The term *puffing* refers to taking the truth and expanding on it a bit. In the old days, some people might have described it as a white lie. Puffing is not truly lying, but it can paint a picture that is a bit more attractive in the mind's eye than it is on a financial statement.

When you receive documents on a building, go over them carefully. During my years in real estate, I've seen a lot of omissions. Surely some of them were honest mistakes, but some have seemed questionable in terms of intent. For example, if you are looking at a building's income and expenses, make sure you are evaluating actual income, not potential income. Also confirm that all expenses are accounted for. If a seller neglects to list the cost of water and sewage services, for example, the property's rate of return could look quite different. Leave nothing to chance. Check out everything.

Perform a historical data search on every property you consider buying. You might find some factors that concern you. For example, say that a building you are investigating is pulling rents of $650 a month in a neighborhood where rents for similar units in other buildings are as low as $550. Investigate the difference. There may be a plausible excuse, but it may be that the property owner was lucky enough to fill the building with tenants willing to pay higher rents that will not hold up over time. Don't take anything for granted. Keep your future in your own hands. Work with brokers, have them work for you, but don't slack off. You are responsible for your own good fortune.

CHAPTER 17

You Can Be Your Own Broker

Is being your own broker a good idea? The same saying that goes "lawyers who represent themselves have fools for clients" might apply to anyone wishing to act as his own real estate broker. However, it can be very beneficial to work as your own broker—but only when you are a qualified real estate expert. If you want to be a licensed broker, you will have to invest some time in real estate courses or reading, and you will need to pass a state-issued licensing exam, but the rewards may be worth the effort. For example, if you are a licensed broker, you can earn a commission when you buy a property for yourself. No law prevents brokers from acting in their own best interests. Laws do, however, require investors to disclose when they are licensed brokers as well as parties to real estate offerings. Being a licensed broker with access to the MLS and other business-related benefits also can help you find better deals faster. And being your own broker means depending on yourself rather than a commission-paid stranger to make solid deals and ensure your financial future. Certainly these are advantages to representing yourself, and you don't need a license to do it, but disadvantages also are numerous.

People who work without brokers sometimes are compared to tightrope walkers who work without nets. Overall, I don't encourage people with a casual understanding of real estate law and principles to work on their own; however, I do support a person's right to depend on herself and to save a few bucks on commissions when she can. The watchword is *knowledge.* If you know what you are doing, do it, but don't think that all real estate deals are simple or that being your own broker will be in your best interest all of the time. Unless you are completely qualified to represent yourself, don't.

If You Go It Alone in the Real Estate Jungle

Going it alone in the real estate jungle can be dangerous. People who do not have the advanced knowledge and skills of experienced brokers are at a disadvantage; however, you don't need a license to sell real estate you own. Neither do you need a license to buy real estate. As I mentioned above, the biggest advantage of self-representation when you purchase a property is the potential savings of commission. But in reality, there may be no savings. Let me give you an example.

For Example . . .

Let's say that as an investor who does not hold an active real estate license, you decide to be your own buyer's broker. You find a building listed with a brokerage for $200,000. A 10 percent sales commission is due the listing brokerage. If you were a licensed broker, you normally would receive half of the commission once the sale closed. Because you are not licensed, the listing brokerage will not split the commission with you. If you can persuade the seller to accept a lower price or negotiate with the brokerage to take a lower commission because no cobroker is involved, you will save money. Most likely, though, the brokerage will keep the full 10 percent and you will have saved nothing. This makes it seem pointless not to use a buyer's broker to represent you. ■

In all of my years as a broker and a brokerage owner, I can't think of a single time when I've cut my commission to accommodate someone who wasn't a cobroker. Some brokers probably do. I have, however, worked with other brokers to lower commissions for both the seller's side and the buyer's side. Trying to get a brokerage to settle for less may be worth attempting, but don't be too disappointed if it doesn't pan out.

Because the only reason for buying property on your own is to save commission dollars, and often it is difficult to actually save that money, generally I don't think it makes sense to work without a buyer's broker. Good brokers can bring you a host of viable deals, many of which you might never find on your own. Having a broker working for you to find viable properties also can save you a lot of time.

Now, if you are *selling* a property, that's a whole different story. In our sample deal above, the commission works out to $20,000. If you act as your own listing brokerage, you can buy a lot of advertising for $20,000. You could even offer $10,000 as a commission to selling brokers and buy ads with the other $10,000. Remember, most people deal with brokers when buying property, so you can use all the help you can get from agents when it comes to bringing buyers to the table. Working as your own broker makes a lot of sense if you are capable of handling your own sales. The services of a good real estate attorney make this process much more viable, and the legal fees tend to be much less than the commission rates.

If you try to sell your own property, you will have to pay for the advertising. Listing your property with a brokerage relieves you of advertising expenses, however, even if the building doesn't sell. By the same token, you have little control over when, where, and how often the brokerage advertises your property if you sign an exclusive listing. You might be better off to pay for your own advertising and enjoy the control of your own destiny.

Perfecting Your Skills as a Real Estate Investor

You can perfect your skills as a real estate investor in numerous ways. Reading books and articles and attending seminars are always good ways to expand your knowledge of the real estate business. Videotapes and audiotapes can move you up a few rungs on the ladder of success. Taking classes at local adult education facilities helps you explore the depth of real estate law and principles. Many educational facilities offer real estate courses for those wishing to become licensed salespeople. Not only will these courses help you understand the ins and outs of real estate, they put you on the track to getting a sales license, which can result in a broker's license and eventually your own brokerage.

Many investors don't take the time to learn all aspects of real estate. They think all they need is money or credit to play the game. True, money and credit *will* get you onto the field, but if you want to win big, strive to learn all you can about the business. Also, getting a sales license can help your profits grow more quickly.

I've had a philosophy in my career: Don't hire anyone to do work for you when you don't understand what that person is doing. Obviously, it's not practical to learn everything about all forms of work, but you can concentrate on elements of your profession and learn all you can about them. For example, I'm not a roofer. When I hire a roofer, though, I know enough to see that the job is done right.

The same holds true when I hire a carpenter or an electrician. Land-lords should possess at least a basic knowledge of the trades and a strong understanding of property management and real estate.

The time you invest in learning about your new business will not be wasted. At some point, you should see direct benefits from your research. Therefore, put in the effort. Go to some classes. Read more books. Learn what you can from the success of others. Don't try to reinvent the wheel, but follow in the footsteps of those who have gone before you and who have established successful real estate careers.

Running Your Own Property Searches

Running your own property searches can take a lot of time. Also, beginning investors don't have access to sources that many real estate professionals do. While a real estate broker might be able to compile a long list of comparable sales in a matter of minutes, the novice investor could take days to accomplish the same work. People outside of the real estate profession simply don't have as many tools available to them as professionals in the loop.

Assuming that you don't have special access to information, be prepared for your property data search to be time consuming. The local tax assessor's office is one place to begin your search. Tax records can show a lot of detail about properties, but not all records in all jurisdictions are the same. In the case of a house, for example, you might learn how many bedrooms and bathrooms the home has and the amount of land the house sits on. The amount of detail varies. The property's tax assessment, of course, will always be listed in these records. It is common for a property's tax value to be less than its market value. Many investors feel that a property that can be purchased for its tax value is a good deal.

Newspapers also are valuable tools during research, but they usually don't document sales prices for properties that have changed hands. It's easy to determine the properties' asking prices, but asking prices and sales prices normally differ. Likewise, landlords can watch rents in newspapers, but rental asking prices are no guarantee of real rental rates. The advertisements are, however, a good barometer of the rental market, so study newspapers in your property data research, but remember they are not sources of fact for rental or sales figures.

If you act as your own broker and attempt to run your own property searches, you will have your hands full. When you have the representation of a buyer's broker, you can request in-depth information and spend your time reviewing the data rather than collecting them. For most investors, this is a better use of their time. Another option is to look for local brokers who have Web sites on the Internet. You can view their offerings in the comfort of your home at any time of the day or night.

Obtaining Distinctive Data

Collecting distinctive data can be crucial to your success as an investor. Gaining access to this type of information, however, can be difficult for anyone without ties to an MLS or another collective database. While you might have trouble obtaining detailed data on comparable properties, you can get the essential data you need for the property you are interested in simply by asking for them. Any property seller should be willing to provide you with all of the information pertinent to the sale.

Let's assume that you are buying an apartment building. You want to know as much as you can about income and expenses. Surely the seller should be willing and able to provide you with all utility bills, all property tax information, and a detailed accounting of vacancies, maintenance expenses, management costs, and so on.

Collect this type of information with a vengeance. You deserve and need as much data as you can get.

Closing on a Real Estate Deal

Putting a deal on paper starts the ball rolling toward a closing. When you deal with a broker, the broker usually provides a boiler-plate contract with fill-in-the-blank spaces. When you transact business without a broker, have your attorney prepare your documents. Verbal agreements are legal, but rarely enforceable; therefore, real estate contracts must be in writing to be enforceable.

Whether you work with or without a broker, the rule is the same: seek professional legal and tax assistance before you enter into any legally binding real estate contract. Even if a broker provides you with a standard purchase or sale contract, have your attorney review the document before you submit it to a seller or accept it from a buyer. Each purchase or sale contract must contain certain elements such as escrow details, contingency clauses, closing date, and financing details. Review the sample real estate documents at the back of this book, but don't use them as legal contracts. Laws vary from state to state. Retain an attorney to draft your legal instruments.

Follow up for a Successful Closing

Follow-up is integral to keeping a deal together. Brokers often take care of follow-up, but if you go it alone, you must rely on yourself. If you are not experienced as an investor or a broker, you are at a disadvantage. Many steps occur between the signing of a contract and the closing of a deal. In fact, it can take several weeks or longer to take care of everything necessary to close a transaction. During this time, a lot can go wrong, so someone must remain vigilant to ensure that the deal closes.

When you act as your own broker, you must prepare yourself to deal with any number of problems and responsibilities. Simple duties might include meeting with property inspectors and appraisers or working with a title company. Normally, follow-up also requires you to attend to your lender as well as a number of other people involved in closings. Obtaining and delivering documents and confirming the status of various activities all make for a successful closing.

Selling Your Own Properties

Selling your own properties is one way to preserve some profits. When an owner engages a broker to sell property, it is customary for the seller to pay a sales commission to the brokerage when the sale is completed. Personally, I feel that it is easier for an investor to sell personal properties than to buy them; however, selling real estate is something of an art.

Under normal conditions, a broker incurs expense when she sells a property for an investor. Naturally, sellers assume some of the same expenses when they sell their own properties. Can you save money by selling your own property? You probably can. Is it possible for the average property owner to sell a property as effectively as a professional broker? It is possible, but not probable. Professional brokers should be better prepared to make solid, quick sales than the average investor. While some investors can handle their own sales work better than some brokers, these investors are the exception rather than the rule. If you have the ability to sell your own properties, however, it can save you considerable sums of money.

An investor who has a good real estate lawyer certainly has the potential to sell buildings or land without using a broker. Normally, individual investors do not have access to an MLS, but you may not need the service if you offer the right terms, conditions, or properties. It's really not hard to make a phone ring with potential buyers. A targeted mailing or advertisements in public media, for example, should attract prospects. The hard part comes when you try to convert callers into buyers.

Some buildings sell themselves; others don't. If you want to complete successful, profitable sales on a regular basis, plan on working at the process. As a brokerage owner, I've enjoyed the saying, "There's a difference between showing property and selling it." I believe this completely. Some brokers show a lot of real estate without selling much of it. Other brokers make few showings and a lot of sales. You could call some of it luck or being in the right place at the right time. Over time, however, it is easy to see that the difference frequently is a result of sales skills.

If you plan to sell your own properties, finding a knowledgeable real estate lawyer to work with should be your first priority. After you retain your attorney, practice your copywriting abilities. Some advertisements draw much more attention than others. Because ads are the most likely way to generate interest in a property, it pays for you to learn how to write convincing copy. You also should study proven sales methods to improve your skills. Many books and seminars teach sale tactics and techniques. Practice what you learn on friends and relatives. Get the feel for talking and acting like a professional salesperson.

Once you combine superior sales skills with an ability to write advertisements with pull, you are well on your way to cutting brokers out of your profit zone. Keep records of prospective buyers who call about your offerings. You might be selling an eight-unit building today that a buyer doesn't want, but he might be interested in the next four-unit building you have for sale. Build a database of investors to mail to. Ultimately, this will be one of your most cost-effective marketing methods.

If you have the time and the inclination to learn the ways of sales, you can be successful as your own broker when it comes to selling your properties. In some cases, this might save you tens of thousands of dollars in commissions. Some properties sell very quickly and cost little to advertise. Others linger on the market and drag out the advertising cost. In almost all cases, however, the marketing cost will be considerably less than a typical sales commission. Your time may be the biggest investment, so make sure you have it to invest. Extra time may mean extra money in your bank account.

CHAPTER 18

Site Visits
and Inspections

Site visits and inspections are important aspects of buying real estate. Until you have a chance to inspect a property closely, you can't make an informed decision to purchase it. Raw land should be looked over just as closely as an apartment building. All forms of real estate require a suitable inspection before purchase. Hundreds of properties are offered for sale on any given day in most markets. Of all these properties, some are good buys and some are bad buys—and it's not at all uncommon for the bad deals to outnumber the good. Only proper research can reveal the real winners.

Some investors make their first site visits personally and perform their own inspections. Other potential buyers hire outside experts to inspect properties before they make their final commitments. In most cases, properties are put under contract with inspection contingencies, which allow the investors to lock up the properties without firm commitments until satisfactory inspections have been performed and the results have been weighed. Smart investors know how to use options and contingency contracts to control properties for a period of time. All investors should learn and hone this skill.

Take an Active Role in Property Inspections

While some investors are qualified to make their own property inspections, most are not. In either case, though, investors probably should hire professionals to assess properties before purchasing them. Novice investors gain peace of mind knowing their properties measure up structurally and physically. Investors with experience in the construction field benefit from an objective opinion. In both situations hiring outside experts can be a wise decision.

This is not to say you shouldn't take an active role in property inspections. Hire outside experts, but by all means do your own poking around. You may uncover aspects of a building that simply don't suit you or your investment plan, or you may ask questions your inspector hasn't thought of. It's not reasonable to assume that beginning investors are qualified to make substantial judgment calls on structural or mechanical issues, but you can oversee the work of the professionals you hire.

When a property inspection has been completed, you may have nothing more than several pages of a written report to review. In fact, require the report to be in writing. Not only does a written report have more impact on a seller, having the inspection recorded on paper is good insurance for you. With that said, a written report can be quite enlightening, but it does not replace good old verbal communication. Talk to the experts you hire. Go over the reports they give you with them. Have them answer any questions you raise. Most property inspectors are honest. If you ask for full details and an opinion, you should get them.

Valuable Property Inspection Tools

Notebooks, tape recorders, and video recorders all can be valuable tools when inspecting properties. The devices offer many benefits to an inquiring buyer. For example, buyers who tour a number of properties in a short time often have trouble remembering details about specific buildings. A videotape of each property's cosmetic elements refreshes the memory easily. Even a voice tape recorder can help buyers organize their thoughts and jog their memories later. A lot of contractors use video or voice recorders to document features when looking a job over to bid it. Some brokers use videotapes as sales tools and mail the tapes to interested buyers.

Video recorders are very common today, and they probably offer the best records of property visits—both voice and visual images. After a long day of touring buildings, you can sit back in the comfort of your home or office and watch the video. Not only will the tape refresh your memory, it may reveal something you failed to notice during your inspection. For example, you might see that the floor in one kitchen is curling around the edges or that one electrical service has fuses instead of circuit breakers. In most cases, you will use the video to determine which buildings contained which specific features. If you can't remember what building had the tile bathroom, for instance, you can check your tape to confirm the building.

As small as modern video cameras are, they still can be offensive to sellers or tenants who prefer not to have their homes taped. However, nearly no one objects to a tape recorder or a spiral notebook used to log observations. In any event, take as many detailed notes as you can.

If you are in the market to buy a building, keeping your facts straight is of the utmost importance. People intimidated by higher technology can get by with a notebook and a pencil. However you decide to do it, document your site visits and property inspections. It can be quite surprising just how often you refer back to your notes during the buying process.

Tip-Offs to Troubled Buildings

Experienced investors know to look for certain tip-offs to troubled buildings. The signals can be subtle. For example, a lack of light bulbs in an apartment building's hall light fixtures could indicate that the person responsible for routine maintenance is doing a poor job. More likely, it means either that someone is vandalizing the building or that tenants are stealing the light bulbs for use in their own apartments. Something as simple as light bulbs can tell you a lot about a building.

Other little things to look for include the condition of the common areas, such as hallways and lawns. If a building's grounds are littered, it's not a good sign. Untidy halls might mean very little, but they could signal that the building's residents have little respect for the property. Clean floors and neat halls generally indicate a better building. Graffiti always signifies problems.

Now check that fire extinguishers are in all the proper places. Like light bulbs, missing fire extinguishers indicate ongoing maintenance problems, at best. Inspect the halls to see whether fire prevention equipment is present. Look in the basement or mechanical rooms to confirm that all of the areas meet fire codes.

When you tour individual apartments, pay special attention to the bathrooms and kitchens. Plungers sitting by the toilets might mean that the drains stop up frequently. Dirty kitchen ranges can indicate a lack of tenant interest. Is the general condition of the apartments good? Sloppy units could signal that the tenants are not the type of residents you want in your building. Because the tenants accompany any building you buy, you probably should seek a building with tenants you can live with. If most of the apartments are kept poorly, however, you might decide to bring in new tenants. This can mean some downtime and lost income during the replacement process. You see how dirty kitchen ranges blossom into shades of the future?

Potential Maintenance and Structural Problems

Sizing up potential maintenance problems is part of any site visit. You don't have to be a licensed plumber to see evidence of clogged drains. Neither do you have to work as a foundation contractor to spot water stains on basement walls. I'm not suggesting that your investigation take the place of a professional real estate inspection, but you might save yourself some money if you can rule out buildings on your own, before calling in professional inspection teams.

When you visit a prospective property for the first time, don't try to soak in every detail. Spend your first visit gaining a general understanding of the property. Concentrate only on the building's features and benefits, and don't worry about duct tape on plumbing traps or water stains on ceilings. Of course, if you see some glaring problems, note them on your recorder or in your notebook. In general, though, spend your first visit getting a feel for the property. Gut reactions often are very strong and on target if you open yourself to them.

If you experience a positive gut reaction to a property, return another day to evaluate the building through the eyes of a prospective tenant. Would you rent space in the property? Now go back with your landlord's hat and take another look. Landlords and tenants don't look at rental property through the same eyes. Once you have completed these two evaluations, go back through the property with your focus on potential maintenance problems. When you have viewed a potential property in these three ways, you are in a better position to make a wise buying decision.

When you inspect a property looking for potential maintenance problems, it's time to turn to specifics. A few examples follow:

- Look for water stains on basement walls and on ceilings.
- Check the cover plates on electrical outlets and switches; black spots may indicate electrical problems.
- Fill up sinks and lavatories, then let them drain.
- Check faucets to see whether they leak.
- Run showers to see whether they drain.
- Fill up bathtubs, then let them drain.
- Flush toilets to determine how well the bowls empty.
- Inspect the flooring to determine whether it's in good repair.
- Open and close doors to see how well they fit; lock and unlock doors to check the mechanisms.
- Turn on lights to see whether they all work; inspect the electrical service.
- If the building is old and has a fuse box, look for spare fuses. Too many spares could indicate electrical problems.
- Look for stains from water leaks on cement floors.
- Open and close windows to see that they function properly.

Basically, you should go through every room of the building inspecting all that you have the ability to evaluate. Take notes of your findings. If the building passes your test and you decide to purchase it, call in professional inspectors to look for trouble you may have missed.

Structural Problems

Structural problems can be difficult to locate and expensive to repair. Buying a building that suffers from structural problems can be all it takes to ruin an investor's career. Most investors are not qualified to identify a lot of structural problems. This is why you should hire a professional inspection team to go over every building you consider buying. It's possible that you might spot some structural problems on your own, but don't count on your own ability to make sure a building is not subject to expensive structural deficiencies.

If you want to attempt your own search for structural problems to rule out a building before you spend money on professionals, you will need a pair of coveralls, a flashlight, gloves, a screwdriver and some other basic tools. Acting as your own inspector means looking for everything from termite damage to roof leaks. To do this you must crawl under the building and into attics to uncover structural problems.

Start your inspection in the basement or crawlspace. Use your screwdriver to probe sills and joists to determine whether the structural members have rotted or have been damaged by wood-ingesting insects. If the joists are peppered with little holes, it probably means that powder-post beetles have been feasting on them. Mud tunnels on the foundation wall usually means termites are present.

Inspect the subflooring from below. If it's black, there is probably a water leak somewhere above. Do you see any cracks in the foundation? A lot of mold or fungi under the floor indicates a moisture problem, as can peeling paint on the building's exterior. Visually inspect all support timbers. Bowed timbers suggest a problem.

When you finish under the building, go to the attic. Look to see whether the roof sheathing shows any sign of water damage. Beware of small sawdust piles on the attic floor. This sign of wood-ingesting insects may mean that the building must be covered with a special tent and fumigated. Are the rafters or trusses in good shape? Do you see any sagging in the attic insulation? Be careful when you investigate attics; stepping in the wrong spot can cause you to crash through a ceiling—another reason to leave structural inspections to the experts.

Outdoor Features Affect a Building's Value

Outdoor features can have an impact on a building's value. The first thing to look for is the upkeep of the grounds. Well-maintained lawns and shrubs may indicate that the rest of the building is in good repair. When the building's grounds are littered, it may mean that the tenants have no respect for the property—a bad sign. However, the tenants may have nothing to do with the trashy exterior; neighborhood residents might be the cause of the litter. Nevertheless, grounds in poor condition could be a red flag.

A building's greenery is not all you should evaluate. The parking lot is another important concern. Is it in good shape overall? How long will it be before the parking area must be upgraded? Does the lot appear large enough to accommodate all of the tenants? Parking lots can be major expenses. Especially if you buy commercial property, the parking lot can cost a small fortune to maintain.

Look for security lights when you inspect a building's exterior. If the property is equipped with lights, come back after dark to see whether the lights work. Examine the exterior windows and doors. Are they in good shape, or have they been kicked, pried, or otherwise manipulated? Check the building for fire escapes and code violations. If you are not familiar with code requirements, buy a code book from the local code enforcement office and study it, or hire a professional to perform this evaluation for you. If the property you are inspecting has a swimming pool, tennis courts, or other exterior amenities, look them over closely and have them inspected by professionals. The upkeep on exterior amenities can take a big bite out of a landlord's profit.

Problems Equal Negotiating Power

If you find problems with a building, you can use the deficiencies to your advantage. The problems give you justification for offering a lower purchase price, especially when you provide specific reasons for your offer. Most sellers are reasonable about repairs needed, assuming they did not take the repairs into consideration when they priced their properties for sale.

Because any defect might help lower the purchase price, keep a detailed list of every complaint that you or your inspectors turn up. Missing light bulbs is hardly worth using as a negotiating tool, but the lack of a fire escape or cracks in a paved parking lot could well be worth a considerable price reduction. In some cases, the price break you get offsets the actual cost of repairs. But some conditions used as pricing prods may not have to be fixed or may be things you can fix yourself. This can result in actual money in your pocket or at least a smaller mortgage.

Another good reason for documenting every item you find to be unsatisfactory is that the process helps you evaluate a building for purchase. If you have one building with a four-page list of problems and another similar building with no problems, you probably can make a quick decision about which building to buy. The time you spend examining buildings is not wasted, even if you do not buy the properties. In fact, the effort can save you thousands of dollars—both on properties you purchase and properties you don't purchase because of your investigations. Take the time to inspect all potential purchases closely and record your findings and you are much more likely to be a successful investor.

CHAPTER 19

Assessing Potential Investments

It's possible for 100 investors to look at the same property with 100 different points of view. Not all investors have the same goals. While it's true that most investors are motivated by money, their needs for cash vary, as can their desires for how they ultimately obtain the money. Every investor must personally assess any potential purchase. Real estate must be chosen based on criteria that meet a specific investment plan. If you are looking for quick-flips and I'm looking for retirement property, for example, we may not be interested in the same properties. What would make you jump to a purchase might put me off. Learning how to assess a potential investment is something all wise investors take the time to do.

It's not a bad idea to hire consultants to help you in your assessment work, especially in the beginning of your career as an investor. Finding a good consultant or broker can be just the springboard you need to get off to a grand start in real estate. However, you may discover that consultants and brokers don't share your personal feelings for properties. At certain times, gut reactions work best, and people you hire may not be in tune with you enough to offer you the best advice. Still, professional advice never hurts. You don't have to take it, but you should at least listen to it and consider its value.

The assessment of an investment can be fairly simple. Some investors simply look at profit-and-loss statements for the last few years and make a decision. Other investors want more data to sift through. Having too much information to dig through can be almost as bad as not having enough, though. To make the most of your time and to protect yourself, you need a plan. Once you have a system for investment analysis, you are more likely to make greater profits from your investments.

Narrowing the Field of Potential Properties

Narrowing the field of potential properties to buy can be daunting, but it doesn't have to be. Start by setting parameters within which you will work. For example, an investor interested in apartment buildings could set the following criteria:

- No one-bedroom apartments
- No buildings with electric heat
- No buildings with fewer than 6 units or more than 12 units
- No buildings without public water and sewer services
- No buildings more than 30 minutes from home
- No buildings higher than two stories
- No buildings without paved parking areas

You can set up the rules for purchase any way you like. Establish your stipulations before beginning your property searches and give the brokers you work with copies of your buying requirements. Refuse to look at any building that doesn't fit the profile. The time you save with this technique can be substantial, and your time may well be one of your most valuable assets.

When you outline the types of properties that suit you, don't leave any gray areas. If you hedge on issues, you might just as well forget the screening process. Define your needs and desires, and stick to them. If you require that sellers be willing to hold paper as a second mortgage, for example, insist on it. When you don't want a property that has a swimming pool, eliminate such properties from your search grid. Weeding out the types of properties that you don't want before you start looking is the best way to narrow the field of potential properties to buy.

Demographic Studies: Do You Need Them?

Demographic studies can tell you a lot about an area—especially when you invest in certain types of property. If you are purchasing or building a shopping center, for example, a strong demographic study can be very helpful. Someone thinking of opening a restaurant also might benefit from demographics. Investors in convenience stores might well want both demographic studies and traffic counts to help them determine the properties' potential incomes. Buying a large apartment building to convert to condos could easily justify the expense of a customized demographic study, but buying a car wash might not. If you are buying a duplex or an apartment building, however, a study of demographics will not be of as much importance. For most investors, reliable, first-hand views of an area reveal enough about the demographics.

Let's talk about apartment buildings for a moment. Assume that you want to buy a six-unit building in a neighborhood you are not familiar with. Several buildings are up for sale. Some of them contain one-bedroom apartments, while others offer mixtures of two-bedroom and three-bedroom units. Does your choice have anything to do with demographics? Of course, it does.

For one thing, one-bedroom apartments tend to have higher turnover rates than larger apartments. Most investors consider this to be a negative point, but if you like annual turnover so that you can boost rental rates easier and more often, you might want the small units. Will you be able to rent the small units, though? Look at the neighborhood's population. If the community is full of children, one-bedroom apartments probably will be a problem. Families require larger units, and single adults may not want to live in an area teeming with kids. Maybe that's why the building is up for sale. If the area is home to a lot of singles or couples without children, however, the one-bedroom units might be a wise decision.

Any time you consider purchasing an apartment building, drive through the neighborhood at different times of day. Park on the street in various locations, and just watch. By observing the neighborhood, you get a feel for vandalism, the income ranges of people living in and using the area, police activity, and more. This personal inspection is just as good as a demographic report, and it costs much less.

Always learn about the areas in which you invest. Sometimes you need demographic studies to gather information, but rarely for average investments. Unless you are getting into commercial real estate, a customized demographic report probably is unnecessary. Invest your time, and save your money. What you see with your own eyes probably will tell you much more than a few sheets of paper covered with numbers.

Crunching a Property's Numbers

Crunching numbers is what some investors enjoy most. I must admit, I myself am an avid number cruncher. Seeing how the numbers work in a wide variety of situations relaxes me. On the other hand, I know investors who are obsessed with numbers and building spreadsheets. One land developer I worked with spent hours each day plugging in numbers and printing out spreadsheets. The walls of his office were covered with green-bar computer paper. Finding numbers that work is important, but you must not allow yourself to become so consumed with the results that you fail to take care of your other responsibilities as an investor.

Investors who despise running numbers—and there are some—usually hire analysts to produce financial reports. Many other investors do their own number crunching. In some cases, the complexity of a task might require the services of a CPA, but for most average investments you probably can do the projections yourself. The value of a spreadsheet is related directly to the quality of the information used to create it. If your numbers are wild guesses, you can't depend too heavily on your reports. However, when you enter solid numbers, the reports you get can be your map to greater wealth.

The many types of investments available require many different strategies. This can make running the numbers confusing. For example, the process used to project the profitability of a land deal where a subdivision will be created is very different from running the numbers to determine how profitable a triplex might be. Putting numbers together for a small apartment building is pretty easy. Doing the same for a shopping center or a large condo project is not so simple. Therefore, the first thing you must decide is whether you have the ability to generate your own numbers. If you feel nervous about the job, hire an expert to help you. The chances are good that once you see how the pros do it a few times, you will be able to assume more of the responsibility yourself.

When you build a spreadsheet, you must account for all income and expenses, including both hard and soft costs. A hard cost is an expense for something like replacement windows, a new water heater, or a new roof. Soft costs cover such things as building permits, inspection fees, surveys, and so forth. Many investors get a tainted picture of their potential profit because they fail to include all of their expenses. Not only can this be disappointing, it can be disastrous to a profit picture.

When factoring in expenses, you have a lot to consider, including:

- All costs of borrowing money if you are financing the property
- Real estate taxes
- Utility bills
- Property maintenance
- Vacancy rates
- Professional property management
- Insurance
- Engineering and survey costs
- Expenses for building permits, inspections, and other fees

Now for the fun part. Very few investors fail to account for their known income from a property deal, and they sometimes overestimate their anticipated income. Be conservative when you lay out projected income. You will be happy to make more than you thought you would, but the results may not be so pleasing if you make less than you project. Try to work with known figures whenever possible, and limit your guessing to areas where you simply have no other choice. In summary, account for every possible expense when you build your spreadsheet. Once you feel you have all the bases covered, deduct some more of your projected profit. You want to build a conservative barrier against cost overruns. It's fine to be aggressive in your mind, but be conservative in your actions if you want to survive the business for many years to come. Make sure your risks are calculated so that you can endure any losses you might encounter.

Talk to Real Estate Players

Talk is cheap, so they say, but not when it comes to real estate investing. Especially as a novice investor you should talk to everyone you meet—brokers, appraisers, tenants, other landlords—to get a feel for the industry. Real estate is a competitive business, but many of the players are more than happy to talk about their deals once they are completed. Bragging is big fun for a lot of investors. Even when investors fall into bad deals, they often like to complain about what went wrong. You can learn a lot from talking to others within the business.

Some investors don't enjoy the social scene. Attending events specifically to talk with fellow investors just doesn't appeal to certain people. If you fall within this group, consider hiring people to talk to. Appraisers normally consult with investors for an hourly fee. Brokers generally give their time to investors in hopes of making money on a sale. Tenants in buildings for sale frequently volunteer information to prospective buyers. Other building owners may or may not be willing to talk honestly about their successes or failures. Try to build a network of people you feel comfortable talking to. You can learn a lot from the experiences of others.

Using Historical Data to Make Buying Decisions

Given enough history on a building or a neighborhood, you can make some fairly safe projections for the future. For example, studying the cost of a building's fuel oil over the past five years can help you to project the cost for the coming winter. Comparing sales in a region allows you to make a strong assessment of current market values for all types of real estate. Tracking the rise in property taxes or association fees could be enough to scare you away or help you estimate future increases. Much about the future can be learned from the past.

You can recover historical data from a number of sources, including:

- A seller's property records (utilities costs, maintenance costs, etc.)
- Tax assessor's office (tax rates)
- Real estate brokers and appraisers (comparable sales)

- Property management firms (vacancy rates, maintenance, repairs, similar expenses)
- Newspapers (asking prices for rents and buildings)
- Recorder of deeds (how often properties have changed hands)

Invest all the time you can afford finding out everything there is to know about a property and the area in which you will invest your money.

Combining Your Research

Once you have compiled a number of files containing various types of historical data, you can begin to put the pieces of the financial puzzle together. Drawing from your research allows you to generate a good projection of what to expect from a given property. Of course, speculation offers no guarantees, but historical data can take a lot of the guesswork out of the building decision. Investors who work with past facts to project future earnings tend to be more successful than investors who simply roll the dice and hope for the best.

Building Inspections—
A Wise Investment

Building inspections are an important part of buying real estate. In fact, most real estate investors now insist on professional building inspections before they purchase property. This is true of people buying homes, as well as investors purchasing income-producing properties. All types of properties demand some inspection. Even raw land should be inspected: a survey should be performed; zoning requirements must be checked; setbacks need to be verified; and soils tests might be required, among other things. Buildings should be inspected from the ground up, and their amenities, such as swimming pools, need to be checked for defects. Physical inspections of all property types should be carried out before the purchase of any real estate.

Only a small percentage of investors are qualified to perform all aspects of a property inspection; therefore, most professional investors hire experts. But what constitutes a professional inspector? Does the inspector need an engineering degree? Personally, I'd rather hire a general contractor who has 15 years of field experience than someone with a college degree and limited experience. A degree is not necessary, but knowledge is crucial. Not all inspectors have the

189

expertise to inspect all aspects of a property. In some cases, it pays to hire more than one inspector so you gain the benefit of experts in various fields of construction.

Bringing in Experts to Inspect a Property

Bringing in experts to evaluate properties can get expensive, but you might pay a lot more in the long run if you buy a building that is not inspected before purchase. A professional inspection can protect you from all sorts of expenses. For example, a heating expert might discover that an oil-fired boiler's combustion chamber is cracked and that the boiler must be replaced—at a substantial cost. An electrician might find that a building's electrical service is too small and must be upgraded—another expensive proposition. A termite company might determine that a building's joists and sills have been eaten away by active termites. Any number of problems could turn up, ranging from basement walls that leak to a roof about to cave in. You simply can't afford to assume that a property is in good repair. It is essential that you hire experts to inspect every property you are preparing to buy. Consider the cost of the experts a bargain and an investment in your future. It's much better to spend a few hundred dollars to discover that a building will cost you thousands of dollars to repair than it is to skimp on inspection fees and face a huge surprise after you own the property. As the saying goes, "You can pay now or you can pay later, but you will have to pay to play."

Inspection Provisions

Because inspections can get expensive, avoid paying for them until you are certain you want to acquire a property. Better yet, secure the property with a contingency contract, then have the inspectors do their jobs. When you put a building under contract with a contingency clause, you control the situation. You have agreed on a price and terms with the seller before paying for professional inspections. If the inspectors come back with negative news, you exercise your rights under the contingency clause and walk away from the deal or you negotiate a lower price, based on the problems the inspections turn up. In either case, you have not spent money on inspections without knowing that you have a deal in place and the property is off the market. Most investors agree that contingency contracts are the smartest way to control property without ownership.

I've bought and sold a lot of real estate. As a broker, I've moved millions of dollars' worth of real estate in a year. In all of my experience, I have never found a seller who balked at a property inspection contingency in a contract. The most resistance I've ever met was a tight deadline for performance So don't be afraid to make a purchase offer that contains an inspection contingency. If a seller won't accept your contingency offer, it might mean that the seller is trying to conceal some unattractive fact about the building. A seller who offers a building for sale but is unwilling to allow the building to be inspected should be avoided.

Hire a Reputable Inspection Firm

Finding a reputable inspection firm is not too difficult. If you are working with brokers, they will be able to give you the names of some reputable companies to talk to. Real estate consultants and appraisers also might point you in the right direction. With so many inspection firms in existence, though, how will you know whether a particular firm is first-rate? Let's talk about some ways to verify a company's status.

When you contact an inspection firm, ask for references. Individuals will do, but see whether the company works for banks, insurance companies, and similar commercial clients. Banks, for example, will not likely continue using a company that does not protect the banks' interests. Because banks can have a volume of work to offer inspection firms, they don't waste time with companies that don't meet their standards. Take some time to check the references once you have them.

Determine whether an inspection firm is insured. Obtain a copy of its insurance coverage, and talk with its insurance carrier to make sure the policy is still in full force and effect. Sometimes policy coverage lapses for one reason or another. A contractor who shows you a copy of a policy might not remember to tell you that the policy lapsed last week.

A call to city hall or the town office will let you know whether inspectors in your area must be licensed. If so, ask to see a copy of the contractor's license, and record the license number for your files. Call the Better Business Bureau to learn of any complaints filed against the inspection company. Ask real estate brokers whether they know of the firm you are considering. Most brokers have contact with many inspection firms because the brokers often meet the inspectors at properties to give them access.

Other questions you can ask to help you determine a firm's abilities include the following:

- What are the credentials of the person or people who will be doing your inspection? (It's fine if company owner holds a number of degrees and licenses, but if that person won't inspect your potential property personally, his credentials don't do you any good.)
- How long has the company been in business?
- Does the company testify in courts as an expert witness?
- When was the last time a lawsuit was filed against the company?
- Has the company's insurance carrier had to pay any claims for mistakes made by the inspection firm?

Don't be shy when asking questions. It's your investment on the line, so don't hesitate to get your money's worth when you hire an inspection company.

Types of Property Inspectors: Specialists vs. Generalists

Should you hire inspectors who are specialists in their fields, or should you hire a full-range, general inspector? This is a tough question. In most cases, a generalist suits the task. Many fine inspection firms evaluate all aspects of a building and do a good job of it. However, specialists are always a better choice. Of course, the cost of bringing in an army of specialists undermines your proposed profit zone, but hiring experts in various phases of construction is hard to beat.

As a rule of thumb, I would say that general inspection firms are adequate, and suit most situations, but that specialized inspections are better. The final decision is up to you. However, if you are thinking of buying a building that has been damaged by fire, for example, hiring a specialized inspection team would be warranted. Also, if a general inspection raises any concerns about a specific aspect of a building, you can call in an expert at that time.

Do Contractors and Real Estate Brokers Count?

Do contractors "count" as professional property inspectors? They might, but you shouldn't assume an average general contractor is qualified as a property inspector. Without a doubt, some general contractors possess the skill and knowledge to perform overall building inspections, but the fact that an individual holds a contractor's license doesn't mean she is a suitable inspector. Now, if you pursue specialized inspections, such as a plumbing evaluation, an electrical inspection, a roofing assessment, and so forth, contractors are good choices. In summary, be wary of do-all contractors as inspectors, but don't hesitate to use specialized contractors who hold the right credentials for their fields of endeavor.

Some real estate brokers also perform property inspections. In my opinion, being licensed as a broker does not qualify a person as a property inspector. Some regions of the country have lax licensing laws for inspectors, though, and real estate brokers and others in the field with limited construction knowledge qualify as property inspectors. It is my belief that inspectors should have proven track records and strong credentials as qualified inspectors. Look for inspectors who hold engineering degrees or specific trade licenses, such as master plumbers and master electricians. The inspection process is not something to be taken lightly, and it is certainly no place to cut corners in an attempt to save money.

How to Read Inspection Reports

Reading inspection reports can be complicated. Most inspectors use common language and terms, but if you have any questions, ask for clarification. You are paying for a professional service when you retain a property inspection. Once you receive a report, make sure you understand all aspects of it. If you have any doubts, call your inspection firm and go over your questions. For example, you see that a property's roof has a remaining useful life of three years. If you don't know that roofs generally have useful lives of 20 to 25 years when they are new, the report might not tell you what you want to know: Is three years good or bad?

What if your report states that the property has a 500-gallon septic tank? Is this large enough? The answer depends on the use, but in all cases, a 500-gallon tank is small. Most residential septic tanks have a capacity of 1,000 gallons. An investor who doesn't know this might think that a 500-gallon tank is plenty big—it certainly sounds big. Can you see how a lack of knowledge or understanding could get you in trouble when assessing a property report? This is why you need an inspection firm that will spend time answering your questions and explaining its reports.

Good inspection firms don't assume that their clients have extended knowledge of the construction field. These companies write detailed reports with easy-to-understand explanations and comments. However, if you wind up with an inferior service that hands you a form with little boxes checked off and nothing more, you can be just as much in the dark as you were before the inspection was completed. Before you hire an inspection firm, ask to see some sample reports from previous jobs so you know what to expect. Top-notch inspection firms have sample inspection forms ready that are accompanied by a legend list explaining marks, symbols, and comment sections. If you get this type of explanatory data up front, you probably can rest a little easier.

Using Inspection Reports as Bargaining Chips

Sometimes you can use inspection reports as bargaining chips. If you find defects in a property, you may be able to use the evidence from the inspection report to justify a lower sales price. Not all sellers will be responsive to a request for a lower price based on defects, but many will. It's certainly worth a shot. Let's look at an example.

For Example . . .

Say you are interested in purchasing commercial space on the market for $325,000. The inspection report indicates that the building does not meet current fire codes. Additionally, the building's cooling system does not function properly. Estimates for the work needed on the building total $12,500. Based on this information, you could submit a purchase offer to reflect this amount, but you might lower the sales price by a larger margin because you or your management team will have to invest time arranging and supervising the work. A price reduction of $15,000 might be in order. ■

This type of bargaining often works and can save you money. Never underestimate the power inspection reports can give you during the negotiating process.

Before You Close on a Property

Before you close on a property, have another inspection performed. A lot can happen from the time a property is put under contract to the time ownership changes. For example, if you put a building under contract during the winter, you might find that the plumbing pipes or the heating system has frozen or that windows have broken since your last inspection. It's common for the seller of a property to maintain responsibility for the property until ownership changes. Preclosing inspections don't have to be as detailed as prepurchase evaluations, but they should include a check of all major systems and components.

Going to a real estate closing without a preclosing inspection can prove to be very expensive if something has happened to the property since your last inspection. After the closing, you will be responsible for the cost of repairs. You can avoid this situation with a contingency clause in your purchase contract that calls for a preclosing inspection and that details all aspects of the seller's responsibility to deliver the building to you at closing in a condition equal to or better than the condition of the building at the time of the prepurchase inspection. A lot of investors unwisely skip this step in the buying process.

In general, building inspections are valuable tools for investors. Not only do the inspections protect you, they can serve as negotiating tools. It can cost a few hundred dollars for a good property inspection, but the money is well worth spending. When you consider how much money you might save based on an inspection, it's hard to justify not paying for a professional evaluation. Unless you are an expert in construction, you should retain the services of those who are. Consider the money a cost of doing smart business. Failure to follow proper procedures for building inspections can cost you thousands and thousands of dollars. You have much better ways to use your money, so don't skimp on inspections only to have to pay out massive amounts later.

Financing

Before you even entertain the thought of buying or renovating real estate, you must master financing principles to enjoy a prosperous investment career. Buying and renovating buildings can involve three types of financing. Acquisition financing allows you to purchase a property. A construction or an improvement loan often is necessary to perform the required work on the property. If you decide to keep your purchase, a permanent loan will be instrumental in your long-range plans.

These three basic types of financing can take many forms. They can be obtained from many sources:

- Banks
- Savings and loans
- Credit unions
- Loan companies
- Private investors
- Property sellers
- Insurance companies
- Other less common sources available to the creative buyer

The types and terms of loans available are as diverse as the properties they finance. Traditional lenders offer a multitude of financing plans, including balloon mortgages, fixed-rate programs, adjustable-rate loans, and a wide spectrum of variations on each type. Independent and nontraditional lenders offer even more opportunities. They use every option at their disposal to develop a creative financing plan to meet any investor's needs. Before you can seek financing confidently, you must understand the various types of loans available. Different properties require different types of loans to make them economically attractive.

By the end of this chapter, you probably will know more about financing than many bankers. You will learn what loans are available and how to choose the best loan for each style of real estate. I will explain some creative financing techniques that make conservative bankers break out in a sweat. When you learn to take charge of financing, you can control unlimited amounts of real estate.

Let's start with a brief look at the most common forms of real estate loans.

The Two Most Common Types of Financing: Fixed-Rate and Adjustable-Rate

The Old Standby: Fixed-Rate Loans

One of the oldest and most common types of financing is the fixed-rate loan. Fixed-rate financing is based on an annual percentage rate of interest that does not change throughout the life of the loan. If you originate a 30-year loan with a 10 percent interest rate, for example, the rate remains at 10 percent until the loan is paid in full. For years, this was the standard real estate loan. The advantage to fixed-rate loans is that you know exactly what your interest rate will be, from day one to the last payment. The disadvantage is a higher monthly payment and, many times, more discount points.

Discount points.   Each discount point equals 1 percent of the loan amount. For instance, on a $100,000 loan a single discount point is worth $1,000. In today's banking world, points are a common part of many real estate closings. Whether they are called origination fees, service fees, or (incorrectly) closing cost, the points can number as few as one or as many as six or more.

In the volatile world of money, lenders don't want to commit to long-term, fixed interest rates. When they do, they load the loans with points up front. This provides a quick yield on the money and reduces the lenders' exposure to future losses on fixed-rate loans if the rates escalate. The disadvantage to you is more money out of pocket when you purchase a property. Before you pay excessive points for a fixed-rate loan, however, speculate on how long you plan to own the property. If you are creating a retirement rental portfolio, fixed-rate loans may be your best choice. If you intend to sell in seven years or less, better financing options may be available. Most investors work according to a plan requiring the sale of their properties every three, five, or seven years. In these cases, fixed-rate loans with excessive points waste the investors' money.

A New Era of Adjustable-Rate Loans

Adjustable-rate loans (ARMs) have taken a bad rap in the past because people were afraid of them. Investors thought they would start with a 10 percent interest rate, then face a 16 percent rate in a year or two. In the earliest types of adjustable-rate loans, this fear was not unreasonable. The early versions didn't have annual or lifetime caps. The loan rate floated with the economy and could fluctuate greatly in a short period of time. Many of these early ARMs also used negative amortization to allow extremely low starting rates. You could borrow $175,000, make payments for two years, and wind up owing more than you originally borrowed. This type of loan spelled disaster for many buyers.

In years past, unscrupulous real estate brokers sometimes sold houses with these loans, knowing the buyers' ability to make the payments in future years was highly unlikely. The increasing monthly payment and remaining balance forced many people to lose their homes. During these times, the public turned against adjustable-rate loans. The modern versions, however, are much safer and offer many advantages.

For Example . . .

Consider this: assume you are financing a property for $100,000. You can opt for a fixed-rate loan at 10 percent with four discount points, or you can choose an adjustable-rate loan starting at 8 percent interest with one point. The ARM sets a 2 percent annual cap and a 5 percent lifetime cap. The loan also offers a conversion option you can exercise after the second year for $500. If you plan to keep your property for five years, which is the better loan for your purposes?

With the fixed-rate loan, your discount points total $4,000, due at the time you settle on the purchase of the property. Your monthly payment will be $952.32 for the life of the loan. You will pay $674.54 in interest each month, so in five years you will have paid $40,472.53 in interest. Combining your monthly interest cost and your discount points, your hard financing costs total $44,472.53. If you could have invested $3,000 of your discount points in a conservative investment with an 8 percent yield, you would have earned $1,469.53 in five years. When you add this lost interest income to the cost of your fixed-rate mortgage, your total cost is $45,942.06. How does this compare to the adjustable-rate loan?

Your discount point on the adjustable-rate loan equals $1,000. Your monthly payment the first year would be $733.77. Assuming the worst, we will say the interest rate increases the maximum amount for the second year. Therefore, at 10 percent interest in year two your monthly payment would be $877.57. If we assume the interest reaches the maximum increase in the third year, your rate is 12 percent. Let's say you decide to exercise your lock-in option and freeze the interest rate at 12 percent.

Your monthly payment for years three, four, and five will be $1,028.61. At the end of five years, you have spent $1,000 in discount points and $500 in a conversion fee. Your monthly interest expense has amounted to $39,699.37. Your total hard financing costs equal $41,199.37. If you invested the $3,000 you didn't have to pay in points in a conservative investment with an 8 percent annual yield, you would have earned $1,469.53. When you deduct this amount from your hard financing costs, your total financing costs, compared equally to the fixed-rate loan, cost you $39,729.84.

The ARM, therefore, would cost you $6,212.22 less than the fixed-rate loan, even though the interest rose to its maximum rate each year. In reality, ARM rates do not always increase and may even decrease by as much as 2 percent each year. While it is uncommon for a rate to drop, it is not unusual for a rate to rise moderately. If this had been the case in the example above, the savings would have been much larger. ■

This example should make the benefits of an adjustable-rate loan clear. If the loan has annual increase caps and allows for inexpensive conversion, it is a bargain in a five-year plan. Many types of adjustable-rate loans are available. Not all of them offer conversion features, but most limit interest rate increases on annual and lifetime bases.

A big advantage to adjustable-rate loans is their low out-of-pocket expense. You can put the money you save on discount points to much better use. For example, you might apply the savings to improvements or a down payment on another property. Another advantage is that the lower monthly payments in the first two years allow more latitude for repaying improvement loans. They also help generate a positive cash flow if you use property for rental purposes. By the time the rate increases, rental charges have risen to offset the additional loan payment. ARMs deserve a serious look; they can be the best type of financing for almost any property.

Other Types of Financing Available

Financing Associated with the U.S. Government

Three types of financing are associated with the U.S. government: FHA, VA, and FmHA loans. FHA loans are insured by the Federal Housing Administration. The down payments required for FHA loans usually are less than for conventional loans. Typically, they are fixed-rate loans, with more lenient qualification guidelines than for a conventional loan. FHA loans allow you to finance a portion of the closing costs involved in purchasing a property. Available through most large lending institutes, the loans may be obtained by owner-occupants or investors for properties containing up to four units.

The Department of Veterans Affairs designed the VA loan to help qualified military veterans obtain real estate. The loan does not require a down payment, and the seller must pay all discount points required in the closing of the loan. The VA guarantees a portion of the loan. When the loan is repaid, the veteran's benefits are restored and may be used again. VA loans require the purchaser to be an owner-occupant.

Farmers Home Administration (FmHA) loans, targeted to individuals having limited income, are available on properties in small towns and rural areas with populations of less than 20,000. FmHA loans generally are suitable for investors. This program is aimed at single-family, owner-occupied housing.

Blankets, Blends, and Wraparounds: Lesser Known Mortgages

Some of the lesser known types of loans include blanket, blend, and wraparound mortgages. A blanket mortgage is a single loan that covers multiple properties for equity and security for the loan. This type of loan can be used in creative financing to limit the amount of down payment required to purchase a property. A blend mortgage merges a new mortgage with an existing loan. Normally, the interest rates from both loans are blended to arrive at the interest rate for the new loan. Blend mortgages offer an option in creative financing. The buyer may be able to assume the seller's existing low-interest loan. This merging of the two loans can produce a lower overall interest rate than an investor would pay on a completely new loan.

Installment Loan Contracts Can Be Risky

Installment loan contracts, also known as land contracts, are a form of owner financing that is easy to obtain, but very risky. If a seller owns a property free and clear, he can offer an installment loan to a prospective purchaser. If the seller still owes money on the property, however, be careful. In older note agreements with lenders, sellers could offer installment loan contracts to new purchasers without violating their note agreements. In new loans, this practice is prohibited by a due-on-sale clause.

A due-on-sale clause gives the note holder the ability to demand payment in full if the seller enters into an installment loan contract. In this case, the seller is forced to pay the loan in full, upon demand, or forfeit the property to the note holder. If, as a purchaser, you have given the seller a down payment or made payments to him, you could lose all your money and the property. In an average installment contract, the seller retains legal ownership of the property until it is completely paid for. As a purchaser, your investment is at risk until you have clear title to the property.

If creditors are legally allowed to attach a seller's property for nonpayment of debts, they will be attaching what you thought was your property. Until you are the owner of record, the property may be seized by others as an asset of the seller. For these reasons, be very careful if you consider an installment sale contract.

Construction Loans for Short-Term Financing

Construction loans, also called term loans, are used as short-term financing for acquisition and construction or improvements. Frequently, investors obtain construction loans to acquire properties for rehab projects. After acquiring the properties, the investors must make the improvements or finish the construction before drawing money from their construction loans.

Predetermined guidelines regulate draw schedules on a construction loan. A representative for the lender performs a site inspection of the completed improvements or construction, then advances a percentage of the loan for all approved work. Most construction loans are established with a term of 9 to 12 months. At the end of this term, the loan must be renegotiated and renewed or paid in full. Most lenders expect the loan to be paid when the expiration date arrives. This can be accomplished with one of the forms of permanent financing described above.

Other types of financing are available, but the ones described above are the loans frequently used for acquisition and permanent financing. Now that you are aware of different loan types, let's learn how to use them. The following sections of the chapter deal with implementing creative financing—an integral part of many investment plans. Here are some proven ways to get the most mileage from your money.

Structuring Financing for Various Property Types

Arranging a loan for a single-family home is different than financing a four-unit dwelling. Financing a six-unit or ten-unit apartment building requires a different approach than financing a run-down property. The following sections provide examples of financing for all of these property types.

Financing a Single-Family Home

In our first example, we will finance a single-family home. The home is in livable condition, but because it has the lowest value in the neighborhood, it is a prime quick-flip property. The work needed is largely cosmetic, and the seller is being forced to sell below market value due to a divorce settlement. The average home in this neighborhood is valued at $135,000. The subject property's appraised value is presently $85,000, and you are buying it for $75,000. The eager seller will pay your closing costs on a term loan.

After preparing a comprehensive loan package, you apply for a term loan in the amount of $108,000. This equals 80 percent of the home's anticipated value once you make your improvements. When the loan is approved, the lender advances you the full amount of money needed to acquire the property. You may have to come up with a small cash down payment or allow the lender to place a mortgage on your home or another investment property to secure the subject property. This depends largely on the lender, your creditworthiness, and your track record.

Once you own the property, you begin the renovations. We will say that if you have projected your costs accurately, rehab expenses will total less than $20,000. Each time you complete a significant amount of work, the lender advances money from your term loan to reimburse the cost of the improvements. As we discussed in an earlier chapter, acting as your own general contractor should save you 20 percent or more on the cost of the improvements. If you do any of the work yourself, your savings are even more significant.

When the work is finished, you have the house appraised by a certified real estate appraiser. The bank appraised the proposed improvements and the existing structure at a completed value of $135,000. All certified appraisals should fall within 5 percent of this estimate. Therefore, your finished appraisal should reflect a finished value between $128,250 and $141,750. For this example, we will assume the property's certified appraisal determines a value of $130,000. What does this mean to you? You paid $75,000 for the property and invested another $20,000 in improvements, so your total investment is $95,000. The house appraised at $130,000, earning you $35,000 for your efforts—a handsome profit for a part-time venture.

Now that the job is finished, you will need to obtain permanent financing or sell the property. If you decide to sell the property, you may be able to maintain the term loan until you make the sale. If you must obtain long-term financing, most banks allow nonowner-occupied property to be financed with a 20 percent down payment. If you plan to live in the property, you may only need a 5 percent down payment or, at the most, 10 percent.

Based on the property's value of $130,000 and a 20 percent down payment, the amount you may finance is $104,000. Because you have only $95,000 invested in the property, if you borrow 80 percent of the home's value you will walk away from the loan closing with money in your pocket. You will have closing costs and points to pay, but the financed amount will cover your term loan as well as these additional expenses. You should have a few thousand dollars left over to put toward your next purchase.

Financing a Four-Unit Apartment Building

Our next venture is the purchase of a four-unit apartment building that needs some rehab work. The same basic principles applied to the single-family home apply to this purchase; however, a few differences in strategy exist. With an income-producing property, you must allow for rental income in relation to the rehab process. For example, how much will you lose in rents during the rehab? Will you be able to raise rents after the improvements are made? Will the improvements reduce operating expenses? These are all questions you must answer for yourself as well as your lender.

You can avoid large rental income losses by renovating one apartment at a time. When the unit is completed, rent it out and renovate another. This process allows you to rework the building with only one vacancy at any time. Units can be refurbished as tenant leases expire, or you can move tenants into units that are vacant during remodeling. Some investors empty their buildings so that all renovations can be done at once, but doing the work one unit at a time minimizes lost income. The only good reason for emptying the building is that it is more convenient for workers and the job generally moves a little faster. If you will occupy the property, you may not have vacancies during the remodeling. Leave your apartment for last, and rotate the tenants into the apartments as they are completed. When you finish the last unit, you are already home. Exterior work will not affect your tenants adversely.

To answer the question about raising rents, you will have to do some market research. Check with property management firms and read the papers to determine rental rates in the area. Compare similar properties to establish your projected ceiling on rental income. Evaluate your improvements to help you draw a conclusion on the probability of raising rents. If you are upgrading the bathrooms and kitchens, you should be able to demand more rent. Adding storage, replacing floor coverings, and modernizing apartments also justify a rent increase. If the market research supports increased rent, a lender will be more likely to approve your loan request.

If your improvements include new windows, insulation, or modern heating and cooling systems, your operating expenses should drop. When you show a lender how your changes will reduce your annual operating expenses, the lender will be more inclined to approve the loan. Even if you plan to sell the property, these improvements will make the building more valuable to the buyer.

Financing a Commercial Apartment Building

Our final example addresses the financing of commercial apartment buildings—that is, properties containing 6 to 12 units. When you step into the financing ring for these buildings, the gloves come off; there are no set rules. Commercial loans rarely are sold on a secondary market, which allows lenders to make their own rules. If you can convince a lender your plan is solid, you usually can get a loan. There is little concern over qualifying ratios or private mortgage insurance. It is simply a case of the best proposal winning.

Apartment buildings with six or more units require a completely different approach than buildings with four units or fewer. For commercial apartment buildings, loan approval is based on a building's qualities and profit potential. For smaller buildings, loan approval usually is based on a purchaser's credit history and ability to repay the loan.

A loan officer will want to see a property's operating statements for the last year or two. He also will want to verify the numbers from the owner's tax returns. This information allows the loan officer to determine the net before debt number—that is, the amount of money remaining after expenses are subtracted from rental income. It is this money the investor uses to make loan payments. Expenses could include real estate taxes, water and sewer service, fuel and utility expenses, maintenance, and management. Most lenders deduct 10 percent from the gross income for property management. Depending on historical data, they deduct another 5 percent for vacancies. Once all known expenses are deducted from the gross income, the net before debt number, or net operating income, remains.

Unlike smaller buildings, which rely on market comparison approach appraisals, commercial apartment buildings require income approach appraisals. All of your rehab attention should be aimed at areas to raise rents. Using a market rent study is imperative in determining the viability of your rehab project. You must do substantial research before applying for a loan. When you sit down with the loan officer, it is best to have all your facts and figures in hand. This builds the lender's confidence in you and proves your professionalism.

The final sections of this chapter explore some unique and creative financing tactics. In the single-family home example above, you used creative financing to buy the property without using your own money—and you made an attractive profit. The following sections expose other methods for structuring buyer-friendly financing.

Buyer-Friendly Financing

Who has the most interest in your ability to purchase real estate? The seller. With this in mind, use the seller's motivation to sell as leverage. A seller can participate in your financing in many ways. Some loans restrict certain forms of seller financing, but you have plenty of other ways to prosper from an aggressive seller.

The most common type of seller participation comes in the form of second mortgages, where the seller agrees to hold a note for part of the sales price. Under the right conditions, a second mortgage can make it possible for you to purchase a property without a down payment. If the lender will let you borrow 80 percent of the real estate's appraised value and the seller holds a 20 percent second mortgage, you may not need a down payment. This is a popular and effective way to buy real estate with limited cash.

A seller may be willing to finance the entire purchase price. If no due-on-sale clauses exists and the seller conveys title to you, this is an excellent way to obtain property. Beware of installment sales contracts and due-on-sale clauses, though. Have your attorney advise you on any real estate purchase agreement. Getting the seller to pay your closing costs and points can save you thousands of dollars. The information in Chapter 7 covers life estates, reverse mortgages, options, leasehold estates, and other tools you can use in seller financing.

Consider Creating a Partnership

If you find a super deal but cannot carry all of the financing, offer other investors partnership interests in your find. Try to secure an option on the property before alerting other investors to its existence, however. An option is simply a contractual agreement between a potential buyer and a seller that keeps the owner from selling the property to anyone other than the potential buyer for the term of the option. Usually, the buyer puts up some amount of money to secure the option. If the buyer exercises the option and purchases the real estate, the option money applies to the purchase price. If the buyer does not exercise the option, she forfeits the option money to the seller. When you don't have contractual control of the property, your investor buddies may buy it out from under you.

For Example . . .

Let's say you have a building under option for a sales price of $150,000. Its rehabbed value will be about $275,000.

You find three investors and offer each a 25 percent interest in the property. As limited partners, their contribution is $50,000 each. Their investments cover the total acquisition cost. This leaves you with 25 percent as a partner, with no money invested, merely for finding the property and putting together the deal. When the property is sold, you will get 25 percent of all profits. How can it get any better? ∎

If you decide to use this technique, your partners may resent putting up all the money for the purchase of your found property. However, finding the property and structuring the deal certainly is worth something. After all, the partners would not have a deal if you hadn't handed it to them. No matter how justified your actions, though, the partners may resent being the only money players.

You can protect yourself from this animosity by establishing a corporation and engaging a close friend or relative as a vice-president. (This person's last name should not be the same as yours.) When you find the right property, put it under contract in the corporate name and include a clause allowing the contract to be assigned to another buyer. The clause might read, "Realty Wealth Builder, Inc., and/or its assigns." This clause allows the corporation to have contractual control of the property and to sell its contract to another party. Have the corporate vice-president sign the purchase offer.

Your corporation puts the property under contract for a sales price of $150,000. You then enter into a contract with your corporation to purchase the property for $200,000. You sign the contract personally as the purchaser, with an assigns clause, and your corporate vice-president signs as the seller. When you structure the deal with your partners, each will feel better about putting up his $50,000.

This procedure reduces the risk of irate limited partners. It is not illegal or unethical. You use your knowledge and legwork for your interest in the partnership. With the corporate approach, your partners don't feel abused and everyone gets what she wants. The partners would get the same return without the corporation, but they wouldn't be happy, thinking you got the better end of the deal.

Using Financing to Control Expenses

If you have equity in other properties, you can use that equity as down payment for new properties by obtaining a blanket mortgage. The lender attaches a first or second mortgage to your other properties for security and then loans the money, allowing the purchase of the new property.

A balloon mortgage requires a lump-sum payment at a predetermined date. The loan is an excellent tool when it is used prudently. Although balloon mortgages are risky, they can keep your monthly payments low. If you opt for a balloon payment, set a term at least one year later than you anticipate owning the property. If you plan to keep a property for five years, for example, make the balloon payment due in seven years or upon the sale of the property.

Interest-only loans and loans with accruing, but unpaid, interest also are attractive for cash flow purposes. These loans, similar to balloon payments, must be handled with great respect. Don't put yourself in a position where you will lose your property if you cannot perform on a large payment. Make sure the property will appreciate enough to refinance the loan and make the balloon payment or can be sold before the payment is due.

Determined investors can find money when they need it. It's possible that they will have to pay higher interest rates than they hoped to, but if the investors get the money they need and make more money in doing so, they will have turned a profit. Every profit is one more rung on the ladder of success for real estate investors.

CHAPTER 22

Managing Properties— Without Headaches

Even when an investor seeks only quick-flips, she occasionally comes across a property that offers too much long-term potential to pass up. Other investors buy with the sole intent of creating retirement income and high net worth. In both situations, the investors wind up with keeper properties. When a property with long-term potential is sold quickly, the profit may not be as good as it is when the same property is sold five or more years later, after it has produced monthly cash flows. For these reasons, becoming a landlord is a natural progression for a real estate investor.

Knowing the ins and outs of managing properties means the difference between happiness and despair. Even if you engage a property management firm, you should learn the basics. Whether you own one single-family home or dozens of apartment buildings, these property management principles will keep your cash flow and your attitude positive.

Management Firms: The Easy Way Out

Hiring a property management firm is the easiest way to be a landlord, but it costs money. For starters, the company usually charges

10 percent of your gross rental income to handle the everyday problems associated with tenants and the building. (The amount varies, but 10 percent is the accepted average.) In addition to the fixed percentage, many companies charge extra for services you might assume are included in the set percentage, including fees for advertisements placed to secure tenants, fees for showing your rental units, and rent-up fees, when the firm finds tenants to lease your space. Other charges may apply if repairs to the property are needed. Some firms typically charge for supervising the repairs, 10 percent of the total cost of the authorized repairs. When the property management firm owns the company doing the repairs, this could create a conflict of interest and generate unreasonable repair charges. All in all, depending on your contract with the management firm, you could be spending upwards of 20 percent of your gross income for the firm's services.

Hiring a good management firm has its advantages: experienced managers run your building, demands on your time are reduced, and a stable of tenants, compliments of the management company, often wait to rent your vacancies. This last benefit may be worth a percentage of your gross, but know what you are getting for your money. The amount management companies charge can turn a positive cash flow into a loss. As with most things in life, few people take as much interest in your money as you do. Learning to run your own rentals will save you money, and you will know what every dime is being spent on.

If a management firm offers enough benefits to warrant your business, investigate the company thoroughly. Don't sign a contract with the first company you interview. Shop management firms for the best prices and services. Approach a management contract with the same caution you exercise in a general or subcontractor contract. If you prefer doing things yourself, however, read on.

The Do-It-Yourself Approach to Management

When you acquire a property, write each tenant a letter explaining that the building has been sold and that, as the new owner, you would like to meet with them. When you gather for the first time, tenants will barrage you with questions. The question of rent increases will be high on most tenants' lists. In fact, tenants expect a new owner to increase rents upon possession. When confronted with this question, be diplomatic. Explain to the tenants that you want to complete some research before you make your decision. This first meeting should not be used to inform tenants that you will increase rental charges. (Immediate rent increases can cause your newly acquired property to become vacant fast.) It is a fact-finding mission, designed to gather information upon which to base your management decisions.

When you interview the tenants, make notes on what they say. Decide whether each tenant is the type of tenant you want in the property. If the tenant meets your preliminary approval, move into the paperwork stage and leave a handful of forms for the tenant to complete, including a rental policy form and tenant information sheet. Examples of these and other forms are provided in the Appendix. Make arrangements for the tenant to mail the forms to you within five days. By obtaining the information these forms request, you can make informed decisions about the tenants and rental conditions. If you decide to retain a tenant, you will have more paperwork to plow through.

Lay the Ground Rules

Keep any rehab activities in mind when you make commitments to tenants. If they will live in the property during the renovation, set the ground rules now. Draft an agreement with each tenant allowing you access to her rental unit. Establish the acceptable working hours and how the remodeling will be accomplished. Coordinating your refurbishing with a tenant's schedule can be tedious. Consider this before you agree to keep the tenant in the building. Put everything in writing, and have the tenant sign the agreement. If the tenant's presence will not impede the rehab work you have planned, try to keep the property occupied. The rental income will reduce the cost of your construction financing.

When you decide to retain existing tenants, have them complete new rental agreements or leases. If rental deposits did not exist when you purchased the property, obtain deposits with the new leases. Check the laws in your area, but most likely you will need a new escrow account in which to hold the tenants' deposits. At this same time, you may want to raise rents. Before choosing new rental rates, do some market research on comparable rents.

If you keep your new rents in line with other rents in the region, long-term tenants probably will pay the additional money without a ruckus. New apartments will cost as much as the ones the tenants live in now and moving will cost them even more. The inconvenience of moving is another motivator for tenants to accept the rental increase. If your improvements are completed quickly, you might wait until then to raise rents. Tenants will have no trouble understanding a rent increase if they get improved living conditions in return.

Finding New Tenants

When you are ready to look for new tenants, be selective. Finding good tenants is time consuming, but not nearly as difficult as removing poor tenants. A few tricks of the trade can reduce the time it takes to rent your property. The first deals with advertising. I have found that highly descriptive advertisements draw better quality tenants. The more information an ad contains, the fewer calls you will receive from prospective tenants who want more details. Having the phone ringing constantly is an annoyance and a waste of time. You are interested in talking only with qualified tenants.

When you prepare your advertisements to pull in new tenants, the information you offer should be direct, easy to understand, and appealing. Here are some examples of what you might include:

- If you will not allow pets, state it in the ad.
- Specify the monthly rent and the security deposit.
- Include the number of bedrooms available in your rental units.
- Describe amenities, such as laundry facilities, fenced yards, and off-street parking.

When you show the rental property, schedule as many appointments as possible about 15 minutes apart. Assuming some people will not show up for their scheduled appointments, you will lose only 15 minutes of your time before the next prospect arrives. This is much better time management than driving across town to show a property to a single prospect who never shows up. Arranging a continuous string of prospective tenants also has emotional value. If a prospect who is interested in the rental unit sees a long line of other interested parties, he may be driven to a quicker decision.

Take blank rental application forms with you to all showings, and have each prospective tenant complete the application. Verify references, employment, credit history, and all other information on the application. Some prospects give friends and relatives as previous landlord references—don't fall for it. Bad tenants are resourceful and know how to deceive you. To avoid possible deception, try not to identify yourself and the specific reason for your call when you check references. You might say something like this:

For Example . . .

Hello, this is Bob Roberts. I'm calling as a follow-up on some information provided to us by Dave Farrel. Dave said we could give you a call and you would tell us a little bit about your relationship with Dave. Could you tell me how long you and Dave have been friends? ∎

Wording of this nature throws coconspirators off track. They may forget who they are supposed to be, or they may not realize you are Dave's prospective landlord. Many times, you will get some interesting, candid answers to this line of questioning.

If everything checks out, arrange another meeting with the prospective tenant. Her present home is the ideal place for this rendezvous because it gives you the opportunity to see how she lives. Don't give the tenant enough time to alter her living habits, though. Go to the appointment with all your prerental forms, including a rental policy form, a property description, and even a change of address form, which often is available for free from the post office and utility companies. Bring a copy of the lease, but keep it separate from the other forms. If you don't like the prospective tenant's housekeeping habits, ask her to review the rental policy form and mail it back to you. This gives you a reason for being there, without committing you to signing a lease with the prospect on the spot.

If the prospective tenant meets your approval, have her fill out the lease as well. You can do this immediately or allow the prospect to mail the form back to you. The lease form lays down the law and makes your intentions known. This saves both you and the tenant from misunderstandings and frustration down the road. If the tenant is unwilling to meet the conditions of the rental, you can part company before the tenant ever signs the lease. This is an integral step to building a solid rental relationship.

Keeping Good Tenants

Once you find a good tenant, it is imperative you retain the tenant. Good tenants make property management easy, and they are worth extra effort to keep. If the terms of their tenancies are clear, you should not have major problems with responsible residents. When small problems arise, respond to the tenants' requests. If a faucet is dripping, for example, fix it immediately. You will save money on your water bill and make the tenant happy.

While it is important to respect good tenants, it is also important to maintain arm's-length relationships. Don't get involved with tenants on a personal level. Follow standard social protocol, but don't become buddies. You must maintain control at all times. Never engage in activities with tenants that are not related to the rental property. If you get too friendly, you will not be able to enforce your rules as effectively.

Even after extensive investigation and what you believe to be sound judgment calls, you may find yourself cursed with unsavory tenants. Typically, these occupants fall into two categories: the late-payment group and the rules-don't-matter group. Beware of tenants who no longer pay their rent on time due to financial distress or lack of concern. It starts a week in arrears, then two, and before you know it they are a month behind. Yes, your lease is a legal document that binds them to pay in accordance with the lease terms, but when tenants ignore those terms, you must take additional steps. You may find it necessary to issue a notice to pay rent as a preliminary step toward eviction. Eviction laws vary from state to state and should be discussed with an attorney before you pursue this course of action.

The group that blatantly ignores stipulations in the lease or rental policy is much more difficult to deal with. Often, you will not even be aware of their infractions unless you visit the property. Suddenly, you discover they have dogs, cats or even pigs living with them in the apartments, not to mention junked cars in the parking lot and a trash pile the size of Mt. Everest. Deliver a 30-day notice to perform covenant to these tenants immediately.

Eviction is the ugliest word in property management because removing problem tenants is aggravating and costly. The best approach to this problem is to avoid it. Following the advice in the last section should limit your exposure to the bad guys, but you still may get stuck with one now and then. If you find yourself in a combat position, maintain your composure. Before taking any action, consult an attorney. Tenants have long lists of rights; you don't want to violate any of them. Follow your attorney's advice, and try to negotiate a friendly departure. Listen to the tenant's grievances and consider meeting his demands. Sometimes a small compromise can defuse a volatile situation. Do whatever you can legally to avoid an extended eviction. If you can buy the tenant out of the building, you may be money ahead. I know this probably goes against your grain. You are paying a tenant to leave when he likely owes *you* money. Put these emotions aside, however, and look at the situation through business eyes. The cost of a full-blown eviction is considerable.

Aside from being costly, evictions also can take months to perform. During this time, you endure a bad tenant and probably no rental income. Add to this attorney fees, possible countersuit expenses, and lost time from work, and your cost to remove a renegade tenant easily could top $5,000. When the tenant leaves you with no other options, though, depend on your attorney to remove the occupant from your property legally.

When the time comes for a tenant to move, whether due to an eviction or an expired lease, get involved in the process. Being present to inspect the property promptly benefits both you and the tenant. A thorough rental policy form requires tenants to provide you with punch lists when they move in. Refer to this list now, and note any specific damages that have occurred since that time. This process reduces disagreements over damages. The tenant receives her refundable security deposit faster, and you notice problems sooner.

Insurance—A Cost of Doing Business

Insurance is a word that may send chills down your spine. Despite the high premiums, though, you can't afford to operate without it. Insurance is a cost of doing business and a necessity in the rental profession. In fact, in this world of lawsuit-happy individuals, the more coverage you have, the safer you are. Today's tenants may try to make their fortunes by taking yours in a lawsuit. Therefore, let's review the various types of insurance and their place in a real estate enterprise.

Fire insurance.   Fire insurance is pretty self-explanatory. It protects you from losses incurred from fire damage. If your property is financed, the lender will require fire insurance coverage in an amount at least equal to the loan amount. The lender stipulates itself as the beneficiary of benefits until the loan is satisfied. If the proceeds from the insurance claim exceed the loan's pay-off amount, you are entitled to the remaining money.

In addition to the minimum required coverage, you should obtain insurance to protect your equity. Don't try to overinsure your building. With replacement cost insurance, you will be awarded only enough money to replace the building. You cannot insure the building for an extra $50,000, say, and pocket the additional money if a fire damages your property. When determining how much fire insurance you need, don't include the land value in your cost estimates. Land is not a factor in fire insurance; it will be there when the smoke clears.

Investigate extended coverage for your fire insurance policy. For a slightly higher premium, you can benefit from a variety of coverages, including:

- Falling trees
- Hail
- Glass breakage
- Vandalism
- Freeze damage
- Explosion
- Ruptured plumbing
- High winds

Flood and earthquake insurance.   A property owner rarely purchases flood insurance unless the real estate is situated in a flood zone or on a flood plain. The same applies to earthquake insurance and fault lines. If you feel that floods, earthquakes, or other unusual perils endanger your investment, consult your insurance agent; otherwise, you normally will not require these types of specialized insurance.

Loss-of-rents insurance.   Loss-of-rents insurance could benefit any landlord. The policies vary in content and conditions, but basically if your rental units become uninhabitable, the policies guarantee some retribution from the insurance company. In a serious case, such as a fire, loss-of-rents insurance can save your property and your credit rating. Investigate the types of coverage available, and evaluate the benefits each offers.

Personal property insurance.   A policy covering your belongings may be in order if you keep lawn care equipment, tools, or other possessions on site. Your homeowner's insurance may not cover the personal property. Premiums for personal property insurance do not amount to much, and you will be glad you have it if the worst happens.

Mortgage insurance.   Mortgage insurance is mostly a thing of the past. The purpose behind this coverage is to satisfy the loan on your property if you die before it is paid off. These policies carry steep premiums and often are cost prohibitive. You can achieve the same result with an inexpensive decreasing-term life insurance policy. This method leaves your heirs with a choice: They can satisfy the mortgage or use the pay-off in some other way.

Title insurance.   Most lenders require title insurance to protect against claims from unidentified, alleged owners of a property. A title inspection must be performed before this insurance is issued. The title searcher looks for liens, attachments, old and outstanding loans, and a chain of title. The searches are very effective, and problems rarely arise after title insurance is issued.

If an old and undiscovered heir claimed ownership of your property, she could be granted possession. The same is true of old, but perfected, liens, judgment attachments, and related clouds of title. Any outstanding lien or judgment can cloud a title so that the property may not be marketable without added title insurance. The title insurance cannot guarantee you will not lose possession of the property; it is designed to reimburse you if the property is lost. When the property is financed, the lender is the first beneficiary. After the loan is satisfied, you receive the residual money.

Liability insurance.   You cannot afford to own property without liability insurance. Liability insurance protects your assets from a multitude of lawsuits. It ensures that a person who falls on your icy sidewalk will not take your personal residence in a lawsuit. It means that loose shingles blowing off your building onto a classic Corvette will not put you in debtor's prison. Liability coverage protects you and your assets from any conceivable eventuality.

When shopping for liability insurance, look for quality coverage. Demand the best, and buy enough insurance to cover potential losses. With most insurance carriers, a million-dollar policy will not cost much more than a quarter-million-dollar policy. You may have trouble envisioning being sued for more than a few hundred thousand dollars. Today's legal system, however, encourages people to exploit the smallest liability claim. If someone is permanently crippled or killed on your property, you could face a massive lawsuit. Don't gamble everything you have worked for to save a few dollars on insurance.

Maintain Good Records

Efficient recordkeeping will make your job as a landlord significantly easier. Endeavor to build strong paper trails on all of your management related expenses. This means your files must be organized and accurate (a real plus at tax time). Don't treat your rental endeavor as a hobby. Managing income property is a business—even if you enjoy it! Without precise, orderly records, you will not realize the profits you deserve.

accrued interest Earned but unpaid interest (example: a loan is designed to have accrued interest, to be paid at maturity). Interest builds throughout the loan term and is paid in a lump sum on the date the loan becomes due in full.

acquisition cost The sales price and all associated fees incurred to obtain a property.

addendum A document added or attached to a contract, becoming part of the contract.

adjustable-rate mortgage (ARM) A mortgage loan allowing the interest rate to change at specific intervals for a determined period of time.

amenities In appraisal terms, benefits derived from property ownership without a monetary value.

amortization The act of repaying a debt gradually with periodic installments.

amortization schedule A table identifying periodic payment amounts for principal and interest requirements. The table may show the unpaid balance of the loan being profiled.

annual debt service The amount of principal and interest required to be paid for a loan.

annual percentage rate The effective rate of interest charged over the year for a loan. Note: when discount points are paid, they increase a loan's note rate to a higher annual percentage rate.

appraisal A property's estimated value.

appraiser A person qualified to estimate a property's value.

appurtenance An item outside the property, but considered part of the realty, such as a storage shed.

arm's-length transaction An agreement between parties seeking their personal best interests. Not an agreement between husband and wife, parent and child, or corporate divisions.

as is A term meaning a property is accepted in its present condition, without warranty or guarantee.

asking price A property's listed sales price.

assessed value A value an assessor establishes for property tax purposes.

assessment The amount a municipality or a local authority charges for property tax.

assessment ratio A formula used to determine a property's assessed value, based on the property's market value. (Example: With an assessment ratio of 50 percent, a property having a market value of $100,000 has an assessed value of $50,000.)

assessor An individual who determines the assessed value of real property.

assignee A person or an entity to which a contract is sold or transferred.

assignment A method used to transfer rights or interest in a contract to another party.

assignor A person or an entity that assigns rights or a contractual interest to another party.

assumable mortgage A mortgage loan that may be assumed from the present mortgagor by another party. Note: The person assuming a mortgage accepts responsibility for the debt, but the seller of the property is responsible for the loan if the new buyer defaults on it. The seller can be relieved of liability if the lender grants a novation.

attachment A legal act to seize property to secure or force payment of a debt.

attorney-in-fact A person or an entity authorized to act for another in the capacity of a power of attorney. The authorization may be limited to certain aspects, or it may be general in scope, with all aspects included.

backup contract A binding real estate contract that becomes effective when a prior contract is void.

balance sheet A financial sheet showing assets, equity, and liabilities in two columns, where the totals of both columns balance.

balloon mortgage A mortgage loan with a balloon payment that must be paid in full at a predetermined time.

balloon payment A lump-sum loan payment due at a specific time and in full compliance with the loan terms set forth in an agreement between borrower and lender.

bankruptcy A court action to protect debtors who have become insolvent.

bilateral contract A contractual agreement requiring both parties of the contract to promise performance.

blanket mortgage A mortgage covering more than one real property.

blended rate loan A loan mixing the interest rate of an existing loan with the current market interest rate to arrive at a more attractive blended rate.

blind pool A term used to describe a group of investors who place funds in a program to buy unknown properties.

broker A state-licensed individual acting on behalf of others for a fee.

brokerage A business using brokers.

building codes Rules and regulations adopted by the local jurisdiction to maintain an established minimum level of consistency in building practices.

building permit A license to build.

cash flow A term used to describe the amount of money received during the life of an investment.

certificate of deposit (CD) A savings account instrument requiring a minimum deposit and a specified term. CDs normally produce higher yields than standard savings accounts.

certificate of insurance Evidence from an insurer proving the type and amount of coverage on the insured.

certificate of occupancy A certificate issued by the codes enforcement office allowing a property to be occupied.

certificate of title An opinion of title provided by an attorney to address the status of a property's title, based on recorded public records.

chain of title The history of all acts affecting a property's title.

chattel Personal property. (Example: A range and refrigerator may be found in a house, but they are chattel, or personal property, not real property.)

chattel mortgage A mortgage loan secured by personal property. (Example: An investor buying a furnished apartment building might pledge the furniture for a chattel mortgage.)

clear title A title free of clouds, or liens, that may be considered marketable.

closing The procedure where real property is transferred from seller to buyer, and the time when the change of ownership is official.

closing costs Fees incurred during the closing of a real estate transaction, including commissions, discount points, and legal fees.

closing statement A sheet providing a full accounting of all sources and uses of funds in a real estate transaction.

cloud on title A dispute, an encumbrance, or a pending lawsuit that, if valid, or perfected, affects a title's value.

collateral Property or goods pledged to secure a loan.

common area The area of a property all tenants or owners use (for example, hallways and parking areas).

consideration An object of value given when entering into a contract (for example, an earnest money deposit).

contractor A person or an entity that contracts to provide goods or services for an agreed upon fee.

convey To transfer to another.

conveyance The act of conveying rights or a deed to another.

counteroffer A rebuttal offer to a previous offer to purchase real property.

covenant Promise or rule written into a deed or placed on public record to require or prohibit a certain item or act. (Example: A deed may have covenants preventing the use of a home for business purposes.)

creative financing Any financing deviating from traditional term mortgages.

deed A properly signed and delivered written instrument conveying title to real property.

deed in lieu of foreclosure The voluntary return of a property to the lender without a foreclosure process.

deed restriction Similar to a covenant, a restriction placed in a property's deed.

default Breach of agreed upon terms.

defect of title A recorded encumbrance prohibiting the transfer of a free and clear title.

deferred payment Payment to be made at a later date.

deficiency judgment A court action requiring a debtor to repay the difference between a defaulted debt and the value of the security pledged to the debt.

demographic study Research to establish characteristics of an area's population, such as sex, age, size of families, and occupations.

deposit of earnest money Money placed with an offer to purchase real estate to ensure good faith and contract performance.

discount points Fee paid to a lender at the time of loan origination to offset the difference between the loan's note rate and the true annual percentage rate.

discrimination Showing special treatment (good or bad) to an individual based on the person's race, religion, or sex.

down payment Money paid as equity and security to cover the amount of purchase not financed.

draw An advance of money from a construction loan to reimburse the contractor for labor and materials put in place.

due-on-sale clause A stipulation found in a modern loan forbidding the owner from financing the sale of the property until the existing loan is paid in full. The clause can be triggered by some lease-purchase agreements. It gives a lender the right to demand that the existing mortgage be paid in full, upon demand. Failure to comply can result in the loss of the property to the lender.

duplex A residential property housing two residential dwellings.

dwelling A place of residency in a residential property.

earnest money Money placed with an offer to purchase real estate to ensure good faith and contract performance.

easement A license, a right, a privilege, or an interest that one party has in another party's property.

equitable title An interest held by the purchaser of a property placed under contract, but not yet closed upon.

equity The difference between a property's market value and the outstanding liens against it.

escrow The act of placing certain money or documents in the hands of a neutral third party for safekeeping until the transaction can be completed.

escrow agent A person or an entity that receives escrows for deposit and disbursement.

estate for life An interest in real property that ends with the death of a particular person.

estoppel certificate A document proving the amount of lien or mortgage levied against a property.

eviction A legal method allowing a property owner to remove from the landlord's property a tenant who has defaulted under the terms of a rental agreement.

fair market rent The amount of money a rental property may command in the present economy.

fair market value The amount of money a property may sell for in the present economy.

feasibility study A study used to determine whether a venture is viable.

first mortgage A mortgage with priority over all other mortgages as a lien.

hypothecate The act of pledging an item as security without relinquishing possession of the item.

income property Real property that generates rental income.

insurable title A title to property that is capable of being insured by a title insurance company.

interest-only loan A loan with terms requiring only the payment of interest at regular intervals until the note reaches maturity.

leasehold The interest a tenant holds in rental property.

lessee A person renting property from a landlord.

lessor A landlord renting property to a tenant.

letter of credit A document acknowledging a lender's promise to provide credit for a customer.

leverage The act of using borrowed money to increase buying power.

lien A notice against property to secure a debt or other financial obligations.

life estate An interest in real property that terminates upon the death of the holder or another designated individual.

life tenant An individual allowed to use a property until the death of a designated individual.

limited partnership A partnership consisting of a general partner and limited partners. The limited partners are limited in their risk of liability.

line of credit An agreement from a lender to loan a specified sum of money upon demand without further loan application.

MAI An appraisal designation meaning Member, Appraisal Institute.

marketable title A title to real property free from defects and enforceable by a court decision.

mortgage banker Someone who originates, sells, and services mortgage loans.

mortgage broker Someone who arranges financing for a fee.

mortgagee An entity holding a lien against real property.

mortgagor An entity pledging property as security for a loan.

net income The amount of money remaining after all expenses are paid.

net worth The amount of equity remaining when all liabilities are subtracted from all assets.

net yield The return on an investment after all fees and expenses are subtracted.

novation An agreement where one individual is released from an obligation through the substitution of another party.

passive investor An investor who provides money but not personal services in a business endeavor.

pro forma statement A spreadsheet projecting the outcome of an investment.

secondary mortgage market A system where investors buy and sell mortgages.

warranty deed A deed where the grantor protects the grantee against any and all claims.

zoning The legal regulation of private land use.

RESOURCES

Online Real Estate Forums

www.creonline.com
Creative Real Estate Online

This site offers how-to articles, money-making ideas, a legal corner, a cash-flow forum, books, courses, news group, chat room, players club, success stories, money sources, and classified ads. The site revolves around investing in real estate and creative financing.

www.timesunion.com
Real Estate Parlor

This site has open forums for all sorts of real estate, business, and economic topics. This is a good site for networking with buyers and sellers.

Information Web Sites

www.realtor.com
Realtor.com

This is a huge site that is aimed at real estate professionals, but that also offers plenty for investors. You can find a home, neighborhood, or real estate professional to work with. Public resources on the site include real estate news, a resource center, a finance center, a place for commercial sources, and mortgage rates.

www.owners.com
Owners.com

This site offers homes for sale by their owners. You can search for a home, list a home for sale, visit the loan center, read reports, check out the resource guide, and so forth. This site is well worth a look.

www.credb.com
Commercial Real Estate Arena

This site bills itself as the Internet's most powerful real estate database. Aimed mostly at investors who become members, this site does offer a public access area. The database contains information on properties that are both for sale or lease. Presently, the site concentrates on Northern California, but there are plans to expand coverage.

Mortgage Web Sites

www.mortgage101.com
Mortgage 101

This site provides a large resource of information when looking for a loan. There is information here about loan applications, appraisals, bankruptcy, credit ratings, FHA loans, VA loans, insurance, second mortgages, refinancing, interest rates, mortgage calculators, and much more. If you are in the market for a loan, this is a sure site to visit.

www.mortgage-source.com
The Mortgage Source Online

Here is a financial site that provides information on mortgages and mortgage rates. The site has an ability to help you find a lender online. There is a service that allows visitors to ask the mortgage experts questions.

www.blackburne.com
1st AAA Commercial Mortgage Lender Databank

This is a site that offers free information on lenders of all sorts. You can search a database for commercial lenders, apply for a commercial mortgage online, compare interest rates, get business loans, home loans, or just enjoy the joke of the day. According to the site, an online commercial mortgage miniapplication can be filled out in less than four minutes.

Foreclosures on the Internet

www.bankhomes.net
Foreclosures On Line

Here is a site that gives you access 24 hours a day to a reported 20,000 listings of foreclosed property. The site boasts 3,000 lenders involved in all 50 states. This site offers a database, books, articles, news, resources, and a section about foreclosure talk, as well as a real estate library. There is a one-time cost of $195 and monthly dues of $19.95 if you want to take full advantage of the site.

www.foreclosuresusa.net
Foreclosures USA

This site lists bank and government foreclosures nationwide. The site explains a bit about foreclosures, speaks of homes selling for as low as $10,000, provides other real estate links, and offers debt management services.

Magazines

Affordable Housing Finance (415-546-7255) This is a bimonthly magazine aimed at developers of affordable apartments.

Business Facilities (908-842-7433) This monthly magazine covers corporate expansion, economic development, and commercial and industrial real estate.

Canadian Property Management (416-588-6220) Published eight times a year, this magazine covers every type of real estate from residential properties to hospitals. The publication provides investors with industry news, case law reviews, technical updates, and more.

Commercial Investment Real Estate Journal (312-321-4460) This bimonthly magazine focuses on commercial real estate investment. It publishes pieces on trends and development ideas for commercial properties.

Condo Management Magazine (508-879-4744) This monthly magazine covers condo management in New England, Florida, and California. The pieces published range from roofing and painting to security and insurance.

Financial Freedom Report Quarterly (801-273-5301) This quarterly magazine is written for both professional and semiprofessional investors. The magazine is packed with how-to articles and is well worth your time. I've written many articles for this one, and the content is always top drawer.

Journal of Property Management (312-329-6058) This bimonthly publication covers all aspects of real estate management. It is published by the Institute of Real Estate Management and can be counted on for timely and authoritative articles.

Managers Report (407-687-4700) This monthly magazine covers property management and condo issues. There are how-to articles, interviews, profiles, new product opinions, technical reports, and personal experiences to learn from. Many investors view this magazine as a problem solver for technical trouble encountered with real estate.

Books

Analyzing Investment Properties, by A.W. Tompos (Prentice-Hall)

Big Money in Real Estate Foreclosures, by Ted Thomas (John Wiley & Sons)

Building Wealth: From Rags to Riches with Real Estate, by Russ Whitney (Simon & Schuster)

Buying and Managing Residential Real Estate, by Andrew McLean (NTC/Contemporary Publishing)

Buying Real Estate Foreclosures, by Melissa Kollen (McGraw-Hill)

Buy It, Fix It, Sell It: Profit!, by Kevin Myers (Dearborn)

Buy or Sell Real Estate after the 1997 Tax Act: A Guide for Home-owners and Investors, by Robert Irwin (John Wiley & Sons)

Buy Right, Sell High, by Robert Irwin (Dearborn)

Co-op and Condo Ownership, by Vicki Chesler (New Your Cooperator)

Fundamentals of Real Estate Investment, by Austin Jaffe (Prentice-Hall)

Getting Started in Real Estate Investing, by Michael Thomsett (John Wiley & Sons)

Goldmining in Foreclosure Properties, by George Achenbach (John Wiley & Sons)

House Flipping for Fun & Profit, by Vic Mittelberg (Sabra Publications)

How to Buy and Sell Apartment Buildings, by Eugene Vollucci (John Wiley & Sons)

Leases & Rental Agreements, by M. Stewart (Nolo Press)

Real Estate: The World's Greatest Wealth Builder, by Carleton Sheets (Bonus Books)

Real Estate Finance and Investment Manual, by Jack Cummings (Prentice-Hall)

Real Estate Investing from A to Z, by William Pivar (McGraw-Hill)

Real Estate Investment and Acquisition Workbook, by Howard Zuckerman (Prentice-Hall)

Real Estate Investments and How to Make Them, by Milt Tanzer (Prentice-Hall)

Realty Bluebook, by Robert DeHeer (Dearborn)

Rental Real Estate, by Holmes Crouch (All Year Tax Guides)

Sleeping Like a Baby: Investing in Volatile Markets, by J.C. Hudelson (Lighthouse Publishing, Inc.)

So, You Want to Go into Real Estate?: The Source of All Wealth, by Maxx Robinson (Cardinal Books)

The Condo and Co-op Handbook, by Roger Woodson (Macmillian General Reference)

The Real Estate Investor's Tax Guide, by Vernon Hoven (Dearborn)

Tips & Traps When Mortgage Hunting, by Robert Irwin (McGraw-Hill)

INDEX